W9-BIS-078

A Desert Bestiary

BOOKS BY GREGORY McNAMEE

NONFICTION

A Desert Bestiary
In the Presence of Wolves (with Art Wolfe)
Gila: The Life and Death of an American River
The Return of Richard Nixon

FICTION

Christ on the Mount of Olives

POETRY

Inconstant History: Poems and Translations
Philoktetes: A Verse Translation

COLLECTIONS

The Sierra Club Desert Reader: A Literary Companion
Named in Stone and Sky: An Arizona Anthology
Living in Words: Interviews from The Bloomsbury Review
Resist Much, Obey Little: Some Notes on Edward Abbey
   (with James R. Hepworth)

A Desert Bestiary

*Folklore, Literature,
and Ecological Thought
from the World's Dry Places*

Gregory McNamee
Illustrations by Marjorie C. Leggitt

Johnson Books
Boulder

Copyright © 1996 by Gregory McNamee
Illustrations © 1996 by Marjorie C. Leggitt

All rights reserved. No part of this publication may be reproduced or transmitted in any form or by any means, electronic or mechanical, including photocopy, recording, or any information storage and retrieval system, without permission in writing from the publisher.

Published in the United States by Johnson Books, a division of Johnson Publishing Company, 1880 South 57th Court, Boulder, Colorado 80301.

9 8 7 6 5 4 3 2 1

Front cover illustration by Marjorie C. Leggitt: Jackrabbit teaches Coyote a painful lesson in a Tohono O'odham story (see pgs. 89–91).
Cover design by Bob Schram
Front cover background art by Molly Gough

Library of Congress Cataloging-in-Publication Data
McNamee, Gregory.
    A desert bestiary: folklore, literature, and ecological thought from the world's dry places / by Gregory McNamee.
        p. cm.
    Includes bibliographical references and index.
    ISBN 1-55566-176-9 (pbk.: alk. paper)
    1. Desert animals. 2. Desert animals—Folklore. 3. Animals in literature. I. Title.
QL116.M4 1996   96-32856
591.909'54—dc20   CIP

Printed in the United States by
Johnson Printing
1880 South 57th Court
Boulder, Colorado 80301

 Printed on recycled paper with soy ink.

for
Melissa

Do not divert your love from tangible things.
Continue to love what is good, simple, and ordinary:
animals and flowers. Keep the balance true.

Rainer Maria Rilke

My heart is moved by all I cannot save:
so much has been destroyed
I have to cast my lot with those who age after age,
perversely, with no extraordinary power,
reconstitute the world.

Adrienne Rich

Contents

Introduction

"History," writes the Bulgarian philosopher Elias Canetti, "talks too little about animals."

Canetti recorded those charged words during the fiercest years of World War II, as the world he had known was disintegrating in a vast wall of flame. But even in the darkest hours of the war, fully aware of concentration camps and firebombings and the other horrors that had swept over Europe, Canetti turned his attention away from human savagery toward a second holocaust in the making: the destruction of the natural world, the end of nature and of life itself.

Canetti spent his youth in the Black Sea port of Ruschuk, Bulgaria, where his earliest memories were of housemaids' tales of werewolves and vampires. His mother had once been beset by wolves while crossing the ice-covered Danube in a troika, and for years afterward she suffered nightmares about their red tongues and white fangs. Canetti, we may suspect, sympathized with the wolves, and he recognized that when their howling came ever more seldom from the hills outside Ruschuk to his open window, the world would change for the worse. It did, and to those who arrogantly proclaim that humans are the alpha and omega of existence, Canetti would later say, "It turns out that we are actually God's lowest creature, that is to say, God's executioner in his world."

As a species, *Homo sapiens* has indeed acted as an executioner in the world, and the toll of victims mounts. At the same time, humans have tried, however imperfectly, to understand nature and our place in it. The result has been a rich literature, full of moralizing and speculation, full of the most outlandish exaggeration and the most profound sympathy. Elements of all these tendencies occur in this classification of animals from the Chinese *Tai Ping Kuan Chi*:

> (1) Those Belonging to the Emperor; (2) Embalmed; (3) Tame; (4) Suckling Pigs; (5) Sirens; (6) Fabulous; (7) Stray Dogs; (8) Included in the Present Classification; (9) Frenzied; (10) Innumerable; (11) Drawn with a Very Fine Camelhair Brush; (12) Et Cetera; (13) Having Just Broken the Water Pitcher; and (14) That From a Long Way Off Look Like Flies.

As the French philosopher Michel Foucault observes, "In the wonderment of this taxonomy, the thing we apprehend in one great leap, the thing that, by means of the fable, is demonstrated as the exotic charm of another system of thought, is the limitations of our own."

Our systems of thought may be limited, but that is part of their charm. An animal perceived by a Chinese scholar of the tenth century A.D. is not the same animal as one perceived by a modern naturalist, head full of thoughts on ecosystemic patches, energy-transfer patterns, speciation, stochasticity. Even among our contemporaries, to say nothing of observers widely distributed in time, you will find a considerable diversity of opinion on the same animals, the same events. Gary Nabhan remarks on that diversity in his anthology *Counting Sheep*, in which twenty writers take a look at one species, *Ovis canadensis*, and come up with twenty sometimes widely divergent views. The differences are even greater among cultures, as Bertrand Russell noted when he remarked, "Animals studied by Americans rush about frantically, with an incredible display of hustle and pep, and at last achieve the desired result by chance. Animals observed by Germans sit still and think, and at last evolve the solution out of their inner consciousness."

The differences do not diminish our longstanding interest, as a species, in the animals that inhabit our world. If we take the beginnings of literature to be the paintings that Neolithic peoples left on Old World cave walls, we will see that animals were our first concern as writers, as keepers of memory. In the same way, our alphabet evolved as a means of counting sheep—and camels, and bulls, and geese—the letterforms changing from pictograph to stylized symbol, but always carrying within them their origins in the description of the natural world: A as in Aardvark, Z as in Zebra. This fascination remains a human constant. In this regard, as anthropologist Christopher Crocker wisely observes, "People are intensely interested in the animals that live around them, and along with that interest and fascination comes the desire to make other living things participants in what the humans are doing . . . through the metaphoric process."

That metaphoric process ranges throughout our literature. In its ancient expression, in the *Epic of Gilgamesh* and the fables of Aesop and indigenous stories the world over, animals serve as moral exemplars, as reminders against gluttony and sloth and envy, as counters toward an ethic of the common wealth and lives well lived. In late antiquity and the Middle Ages, that moral direction continued, but in such works as the *Historia Naturalis* of Pliny and the *Quæstiones Naturales* of Adelard we also see a movement toward describing animals not only as markers in the great chain of being but also as things that exist in and of themselves, a movement that culminated in great medieval bestiaries that continue to exercise an influence, however subtle, on the way we conduct our studies of natural history today.

In his book *Thinking Animals,* the naturalist Paul Shepard observes of those sea-change texts,

> This quaint literature is but a small part of a stampede of animals crowding into human consciousness in the latter eleventh and early twelfth centuries. The popularity of the regular bestiary— the nearest thing to an encyclopedia of natural history—the new zoos in stained glass and stone in cathedral architecture, the animal little brothers of St. Francis, and the first works of a scientific spirit such as Frederick II's treatise on falconry, all mark a widespread intellectual excitement directed to the discovery of information hidden in nature, a shift to an allegorical form of thinking in which the inquiring individual could seek clues illuminating social complexity from the observation of animals. The optimism of that world, with its contagious attention to illumination, light, and vision, is very touching. It is no surprise that scholars become addicted to its history and its charm can be felt across seven hundred years of intervening time when one compares it to the centuries before it, with their grim and pessimistic disdain of this world as opposed to the next.
>
> This outburst of excitement for natural things was preceded by illustrated manuscripts, verbal folktales, the bestiary itself, the continuing survival of pagan thought in the calendar and astrology. But in spite of all that tenacious feeling for plant and animal lore in older peasant custom, the new atmosphere and sensibility to what animals could mean in the twelfth century suggests a revolution in the perception of nature. It is generally regarded as a kind of bubbling to the surface of European spirit, fertilized by contact with the Orient and the recovery and translation of classical literature.

In those bestiaries the reader sees authors thinking things through, trying to make sense of the new animals that exploration and trade introduced to the European mind. This account of the unicorn—probably the rhinoceros—by the thirteenth-century encyclopedist Richard de Fournival shows a profound attention to the fabulous, without a hint of science; yet it has its obvious charms:

> Such is the Unicorn's nature that it is more cruel and difficult to catch than any other beast; and on its forehead it has a horn no armor can resist. So none dares to track and lie in wait for it, save only a young virgin. For when it has discovered a maiden by her scent, it kneels before her with sweet humility, as if to serve her. Hunters who know the Unicorn therefore place a young maid in its path, and it falls asleep in her lap. Then they, who dare not face it while awake, come and kill it.

Is the rhinoceros cruel? Probably not, we would say today, careful to avoid the cardinal sin of anthropomorphism and bent on giving each animal its proper due in creation, allowing it to stand on its own merits, trusting that each came to inhabit its corner of the world for some good reason. (It is hard, even the largest-spirited of naturalists and saints agree, to understand what part gnats, sandflies, and Chihuahuas play in the greater schemes of God and of evolution.) The natural history of our times, having been filtered through the growth of so-called hard science after the Middle Ages, is more self-critical, more aware of blind spots in human observation, more charged with a scientific spirit that doubtless will seem to future generations shot through with a mythopoeia all its own. As Philip Sidney writes, after all, the author of any bestiary, any natural history, is a poet "freely ranging within the Zodiack of his own wit."

In *A Desert Bestiary*, I indulge such wit as I have to celebrate some—a handful, about forty-five individual animals and species—of the creatures that inhabit the deserts of the world. Those creatures are of special interest to scientists because of the adaptations that arid nature has forced on them, equipping them to survive in lands of no water and ferocious sun. Those lands make up a good portion of the Earth, some twenty-five percent and growing. If you study a globe that marks the planet's physical features, as you follow the tropics of Cancer and Capricorn, thirty degrees on either side of the equator, you will see, distributed with suspicious regularity, a brown band of drylands. These lie in the so-called horse latitudes, where constant high-pressure systems separate the westerlies and trade winds, driving away the rain clouds, swirling above the earth to the music of global temperature variations and the Coriolis effect produced by the earth's rotation in space. Some of those drylands, like the Atacama of Chile, the Namib and Kalahari deserts of southern Africa, and the western Australian desert, are the result of cold oceanic currents that divert rain-laden air away from coastlines. Others, like the Mojave and Sonoran deserts of California, Arizona, and Mexico and the deserts of central and eastern Australia are caused by the "rainshadow effect," through which coastal mountains milk rain from the air before it passes inland. Still others, like the Gobi and Taklamakan deserts of Mongolia and China, are simply so far away from the ocean that the winds lose any moisture they may hold long before reaching the faroff continental interior, even what little moisture remains in the Indian Ocean–born clouds after they have scraped over the jagged Himalayas. (In this roster of causation, we will ignore a theory now afoot that maintains that deserts are caused by the backburn of extraterrestrial propulsion engines.)

Harsh as they are, those deserts abound in life, as you will see in the pages that follow. And they abound in the stories that the people who live in them tell about that life; a library devoted to the folklore of desert animals would fill many large rooms. To make this book, full of true statements, outrageous and odd lies, and entertaining guesses about why those animals live the way they do, I have ranged through that library, satisfying my own interest in exploring that vaguely demarcated zone where the environment, literature, folklore, and politics come together, and with an immodest aim: to help construct a history of the drylands that talks at length, and with wonder, about the animals that share our world.

To several people I owe thanks in helping to formulate that grand intention: to favorite authors like Edward Abbey, Diane Ackerman, Mary Oliver, Jorge Luis Borges, Terry Tempest Williams, Bruce Chatwin, Mark Twain, and Ann Zwinger for providing inspiration; and to friends like Kim Long, Gene Hall, Mario Madden, Steve Bodio, Greg Cliburn, Merrill Gilfillan, Joanna Hurley, Robert McCord, Mark Weiss, Terri Warpinski, Natalie Sudman, and especially Steve Topping, Luis Alberto Urrea, and my wife, Melissa McCormick, for encouraging and indulging my whims.

The most important requisite in describing an animal is to be sure and give its character and spirit, for you have, without error, the sum and effect of all its parts, known and unknown. You must tell what it is to man. Surely the most important part of an animal is its anima, its vital spirit, on which is based its character and all the peculiarities by which it most concerns us. Yet most scientific books which treat animals leave this out altogether, and what they describe are, as it were, phenomena of dead matter.

Henry David Thoreau

Objectivity does not mean detachment, it means respect; that is, the ability not to distort and to falsify things, persons, and oneself.

Erich Fromm

We see things not as they are, but as we are.

Talmud

A Desert Bestiary

Ant

Lazybones, go to the ant;
Study its ways and learn.
Without leaders, officers, or rulers,
It lays up its stores during the summer,
Gathers in its food at the harvest.
How long will you lie there, lazybones;
When will you wake from your sleep?
A bit more sleep, a bit more slumber,
A bit more hugging yourself in bed,
And poverty will come calling upon you,
And want, like a man with a shield.

Thus the poet of Proverbs, who, like all desert people, turned to the ant for metaphorical example, finding in its industry the underpinnings of an ethic and a way of life.

Mark Twain, who spent time in the deserts of the American West, arrived at a good-natured rebuttal of the poet. "Science has recently discovered that the ant does not lay up anything for winter use," he remarked, continuing,

This will knock him out of the literature, to some extent. He does not work, except when people are looking, and only then when the observer has a green, naturalistic look, and seems to be taking notes. This amounts to deception, and will injure him for the Sunday schools. He has not judgment enough to know what is good to eat from what isn't. This amounts to ignorance, and will impair the world's respect for him. He cannot stroll around a stump and find his way home again. This amounts to idiocy, and

1

once the damaging fact is established, thoughtful people will cease to look up to him, the sentimental will cease to fondle him. His vaunted industry is but a vanity and of no effect, since he never gets home with anything he starts with. This disposes of the last remnant of his reputation and wholly destroys his main usefulness as a moral agent, since it will make the sluggard hesitate to go to him any more. It is strange, beyond comprehension, that so manifest a humbug as the ant has been able to fool so many nations and keep it up so many ages without being found out.

Ants are common to most temperate and subtemperate biomes of the world, but they are among the desert's defining creatures. What vegetation there is in a desert is partly thanks to the labors of the ants, whose endless digging helps loosen the hard soil and allow plant roots to find their way to water; ants seem to view the desert, at least the patch of it where I live, as a garden, constantly weeding the rocky ground. It is in recognition of their essential role, I think, that so many peoples of the deserts around the world have named themselves after ants: the Green Ant moieties of aboriginal Australia, the Ant warrior clans of the Berbers, and other groups honoring the *anax-forminges,* the archetypal lord of the ants. So, too, does the ant appear in Egyptian tombpaintings and Navajo sandpaintings, in the stories and songs of desert peoples everywhere, fooling, in Twain's eyes, so many nations.

In the Berber creation story, collected by anthropologist Leo Frobenius, the ant is the first humans' chief tutor.

First Man and First Woman wandered around under the surface of the earth. One day they came upon a mound of millet, along with stores of barley, wheat, and other seeds. An ant was running around these piles of grain and removed a grain of wheat from its husk. Then it ate the wheat. The woman said, "Kill it!" But the man said, "Why? Someone created it, just as someone created us." The first man then said to the ant, "What are you doing there?" The ant said, "Do you know what water is?" When the man and woman said no, the ant showed them a spring and said that the grain would be good for them if they cooked it in water. The ant then led them above the surface of the ground and showed them stones. "With these stones," he said, "you grind the grain so that you can eat it." Then he showed the humans how to make meal, and how to make bread, and how to make and tend a fire. "Now we will have full stomachs," said the first man.

The Akimel O'odham, who live along the middle Gila River of Arizona, sing songs about their homeland that, along the way, liken the people to ants, clinging to sticks as they descend into the earth.

Greasy Mountain,
Greasy Mountain stands.
There inside
Green flowers

Cover me.
There inside
Manic is.

Broad Mountain stands.
There below, waters primed to spurt.
And I below there go,
On stick's end cling:
Stick glitters,
then enter.

In Arnhem Land, certain witches are thought to use a potion made of green ants and lizards to close incisions made in victims whose souls they have robbed. Green ants then bite any protruding organs until they retreat into the body, after which the victim is bashed on the head and told to forget what has happened to him. This would, I think, tend to prejudice a person against ants, but the inhabitants of Arnhem Land seem not to hold the sorcery against the insects.

The entomologist Justin O. Schmidt has concocted a rating scale for the bites of various venomous insects and reptiles. By that scale, the bite of a fire ant is akin to a mild shock of static electricity, that of the harvester ant somewhat more severe, as if someone were using a power drill to excavate a painfully ingrown toenail, and that of a bullet ant even more fierce, the equivalent of walking over coals with a heelful of iron nails. Even they do not add up to the punch of a rattlesnake, whose pain rating Schmidt ranks off the charts, akin to sending a scorching bullet into a sensitive limb.

For all their relative lack of firepower, fire ants are a great concern of American desert dwellers these days, and who knows what urban folklore, like that surrounding giant flying cockroaches and sewer alligators, the encroaching fire ants may one day inspire. These creatures first arrived from the South American tropics into the American drylands, having hitched a ride on banana freighters that landed in Mobile, Alabama, only sixty years ago. Their remarkably fast spread is an example of the adaptability of the ants, and other social insects, and cause for a scare, as the Associated Press reported on June 12, 1995:

PHOENIX—Imported red fire ants are making their way toward Arizona, where experts say they are bound to become a common pest.

The insects, known to be more harmful than "killer" bees [*see* Bees], are native to South America and reached this country by ship during the 1930s. They have become entrenched in 11 states from North Carolina to Texas and have spread as far west as the lower Rio Grande.

The ants have a painful and sometimes lethal sting that sends about 25,000 Americans to doctors each year. While improved quarantines have reduced the number of fire ants that stow away on truck cargo brought into Arizona, experts say efforts to keep out the bugs eventually won't be enough.

"There's nothing to stop them from infesting any metropolitan area in the country," said Tim Lockley, a researcher at the U.S. Department of Agriculture's fire-ant laboratory in Gulfport, Miss. "They are surviving in dry climates where they weren't supposed to, and they are surviving in cold climates where they weren't supposed to."

So far, the Arizona Department of Agriculture has been able to eradicate every colony found in the Phoenix metropolitan area. Ants that arrived in the soil of plants from landscaping nurseries in the Southeast briefly infested a few Phoenix-area nurseries and even The Phoenician resort.

The state's main defenses against the ants are inspectors who check trucks at border stations and examine nursery stock from infested states. The inspectors found fire ants on 28 shipments in the first five months of 1995 and on 304 shipments in 1994. Infested cargos other than nursery have included computers, swing sets and frozen chickens.

Fire ants are capable of doing more economic damage than another stinging insect, the Africanized honeybee, also called the killer bee, which spread into the state in 1993. Experts say fire ants could kill as many animals and people as the bee in areas infested with both.

The risk of human deaths from either of the easily provoked insects mainly is limited to a small percentage of the population allergic to venom.

Besides attacking pets and newborn livestock, the South American fire ants kill other insects, birds, rabbits and reptiles. They are attracted to electrical current and have been known to chew through wires and damage outdoor appliances, such as air conditioners.

It is hard to imagine that these fearful fire ants will find a champion such as Albert Schweitzer, who once told a young Sahelian boy he witnessed torturing an ant, as at the beginning of Sam Peckinpah's film *The Wild Bunch,* "That's my private ant. You're liable to break it."

Ants inspire the sometimes totalitarian dreams of social engineers. The Zulu kings pointed to the example of the ants, especially the weaver (*Oecophylla longinoda*), whose tentlike colonies spread over dozens of baobab trees at a time and number half a million individuals governed by a single monarch, as models of social organization. So did the Zuni Indians, who call their crowded pueblo home in the high desert of western New Mexico the "middle anthill." Yet those who see in social-insect societies a model for human societies, as some lesser advocates of sociobiology have suggested, should beware. As Arnold Toynbee writes, "insect societies and Utopias are both patently in a state of arrested development," and we have little to learn from either if we are to live as humans in the world.

That lesson has not been taken in Arcosanti, an experimental community a hundred miles north of Phoenix, Arizona. A garish bit of construction perched on a high plateau, it resembles nothing so much as an anthill, one that mixes the architectural sensibilities of Antonio Gaudi and Albert Speer. Paolo Soleri, the Italian designer and self-styled visionary who has made Arcosanti his lifework, has articulated a weird view of the future that goes something like this: in the coming years, humankind will have despoiled the planet (a likely enough possibility) to the extent that we will all—or at least those of us who outlast the apocalypse—be forced to live in hermetically sealed towers, our allotment a cubicle apiece so small that it would make the denizens of San Quentin riot in a second. The vision is exactly that of a weaver anthill, and inspiration enough, I think, for us to do something about the various ecological messes we've made before we condemn ourselves to living in the empire of the ants.

Bat

The bat, nature's great insecticide, has had a bad time of it for millennia. Aesop tells this story about the perhaps too-versatile creature, which humans have always had trouble classifying into the neat categories of bird and beast, flying and terrestrial creature:

Once a fierce war raged between the Birds and the Terrestrial Animals. The Bat, being of both air and land, remained seemingly neutral in this war, shifting allegiance as the moment dictated. When the Birds led, the Bat joined with them; when the Terrestrial Animals carried the field, the Bat took up their cause. When at last the Birds and the Terrestrial Animals made peace, both condemned the Bat for its opportune behavior, and neither side claimed him. The Bat skulked away and has lived in dark corners and holes ever since, never showing himself except in the near dark of latening twilight.

Likewise, the Chemehuevi Indians of the Mojave Desert tell a story about the bat's failure to fall neatly in step with others' well-laid plans:

Older Brother, dressed in leather armor and holding a concealed bow and arrow under one arm, wrapped himself in a blanket to resemble a small animal. A Great Bird carried him high above a great rock and dropped him into its nest. He was protected from injury by carrying a medicine bundle in each hand. He took medicine from a bag and spread it in the rock; its resemblance to blood fooled the parent bird into believing he was dead and suitable food for the birdlets in the aerie.

He turned one fledgling into an eagle and another into an owl; both flew away. Their fallen feathers were to be of use to the People in their ceremonies. Seeing their empty nest, the Great Birds flew south to find a higher mountain on which to build another nest.

Unable to descend from the cliff, Older Brother begged Grandmother Bat to carry him down; she agreed to do so in return for the feathers in the nest. There were so many feathers that they could fill her basket; she planned to use them in her own nest. As he got into the basket, it expanded to fit him. He closed his eyes in accord with Bat Woman's command, but when he heard a queer noise which aroused his curiosity, he opened them and he and Grandmother Bat fell rapidly. He obeyed her command to close them again and they descended slowly and landed with a slight bump. Bat Woman clambered up the crag to collect the soft feathers for her nest but the wind blew them away. She had no use for the large wing and tail feathers which remained and half flew and half scrambled down the steep rock and gave them to the youth who would turn them into birds which were useful to the People. He would take some of them to his mother to show her he had really visited the home of the Great Birds. Bat Woman hid from him the fact that she had lost the soft feathers, by keeping her basket closed.

Older Brother turned south to begin his long journey home but looked back to see Bat Woman wending her way home on a dim path that led through a dry lake bed which was overgrown with yellow flowers. He warned her not to go through the bushes which had grown on the old lake bed, but she pretended not to hear him and continued on her way.

The aboriginal peoples of the Kimberley Range of Australia, who seem more kindly disposed toward the winged mouse, tell stories of a creator bat who was present at the dawn of the world—one of the few instances in which bat helps shape the planet, as it happens—and of Wariwulu, Batman, who is a protector of the people. In the Gadimargara dreaming, the world is surrounded by bats; when they sleep in their great cave, it is daytime, but when they are out flying they cover the sun, and then it is night.

The bats' play in shaping the world is now in danger. The population of the Mexican freetail bat, to name one prominent North American desert-dwelling species, is in precipitous decline. In some areas, the population has fallen by 99.99 percent in just thirty years; where Carlsbad Caverns, New Mexico, once housed some 8 million, only 250,000 are left, and in the tall caves over Arizona's San Francisco River where as many as 25 million bats once lived, the population is now perhaps 35,000. The thirty-nine other bat species in North America are in increasing peril as well, much of it traceable to the use of agricultural pesticides. With that fall has come a sharp rise in the mosquito population—a Mexican freetail bat can eat upwards of six hundred mosquitoes an hour—and with that mosquito upsurge, in turn, has come an increasing prevalence of tropical diseases in the desert, diseases once thought to have been eradicated, among them dengue fever, which has been striking the inland deserts of Mexico since the early 1990s. With the loss of those bats, too, tequila drinkers will have to look for another libation; bats are the chief pollinators of the agaves from which tequila is distilled. Their loss means the end of an ages-old symbiosis.

During World War II scientists working for the U.S. Army Air Corps attempted to develop a bomb that would release hundreds of incendiary charge–laden Mexican freetail bats over the major cities of Japan. These bats would, the scientists hoped, take refuge in rafters and rooftops and thus set off a huge firestorm when delayed fuses set off the charges. Evidently this bomb was not to have been used on our European enemies, against whom we battled more humanely, and in any event the experiment was short-lived; the bats instead burned down the New Mexico laboratory in which they were being tested.

A Chiricahua Apache elder once told the anthropologist Morris Opler, "If a bat bites you, you had better never ride a horse any more. All the Chiricahuas say that. If you do ride a horse after being bitten, you are just as good as dead." Bats, bombers, and bridles, it would appear, are mixes that just don't work.

Folklore lives by flourishes of the commonplace. Diane Ackerman adds to that of the bat wonderfully by her remark, in *The Moon by Whale Light*, that "their guano smells like stale Wheat Thins."

Bee

The year is 1934. The nation stands stock still with terror. America's fright is not the result of the rise of Nazism, not of Stalin's depredations, not even of John Dillinger's widespread rampaging. No, the country lies paralyzed by the fear of *Latrodectus mactans*—the black widow spider.

The previous year had been a wet one, and spiders and the insects they prey on were flourishing. More spiders means more spider bites, and by mid-1934 such journals as *Scientific American* and *Science* were warning of the threat black widows posed to humans. *Popular Mechanics* went even further, warning that "the spider has become a menace to mankind," and the tabloid media had millions of Americans convinced that the end of our species was nigh.

Well, 1934 came and went, and with it the attack of the killer spiders. Lacking its arachnid enemy, the media went back to worrying about such matters as Father Coughlin and Japanese immigration, saving the next big scare for Orson Welles's 1939 airing of *The War of the Worlds*, when the Martians hit New Jersey. (Japan faced a *Latrodectus mactans* scare of its own late in 1995, when more than a thousand black widows were found in the port city of Osaka. It is assumed that these were stowaways in shipments of tropical hardwood, which Japan is importing in ever-greater quantities. The wheel of karma keeps on spinning.)

Fast forward to 1976. John Belushi and other cast members of the new TV program *Saturday Night Live* are dressed in yellow-and-black striped outfits, toting machine guns and chomping on black cigars. The joke is the arrival of so-called "killer bees" in Central America, an invading force that invited comparison to Alfonso Bedoya's ruffian gang in *Treasure of the Sierra Madre*. Such luminaries as Elliot Gould and Steve Martin join in the fun.

Fast forward to 1984. Central America is no longer funny. Ronald Reagan has warned the country that Sandinista tanks are three days away from the Texas border. In the meanwhile, killer bees have spread northward into Mexico.

Fast forward just two years later, to 1986. Isolated hives of killer bees have been found in California's Central Valley, and the Golden State is in an uproar. "Bee Battalions Mopping Up Killer Bee Invasion," cried the appropriately named *Sacramento Bee*. The bees are swiftly eradicated with cyanide gas, a threat to humans and animals alike.

And now, fast forward to the mid-1990s. The terror has come to the desert of southern Arizona, along with a few pockets of the Texas borderlands. A few recent headlines tell the story: "Africanized Bees Found at Interstate 8 Rest Stop." "Killer Bees Blamed for 3 Attacks." "Killer Bees Pose Biggest Threat to Honeybee Industry, Officials Say."

First, the facts, just the facts. "Killer bees," known in scientific parlance as *Apis mellifera scutellata*, are a variety of honeybee first domesticated in the scrub desert of central South Africa. As a rule, although their hives are small, they are more productive than Italian, German, and the other strains of European honeybees to which they are related. They set to work an hour earlier than other bees, are more disease-resistant, lay more eggs, and yield more and better honey for less trouble on a beekeeper's part.

For that very reason, in 1956 the Brazilian government commissioned an emigré professor, an Englishman named Warwick Kerr, to introduce the bees to South America. At the time Brazil ranked forty-seventh among the world's honey-producing countries; with the arrival of the new variety, that country's ranking quickly rose to seventh. (Much of the honey we eat in this country comes from Brazil.) Kerr lost favor in 1964, when he protested publicly against the then–military government's excesses, and he spent time in jail for his trouble. In 1969 he was again arrested, this time for protesting Brazilian soldiers' raping and torturing a nun.

The Brazilian government was not pleased. To cast doubt on Kerr's credentials as a scientist, its representatives portrayed him in court as a kind of Frankenstein doctor bent on mayhem. The lurid newspaper stories that followed touched off a panic, proclaiming that Kerr had been training his imported Africans to be "killer bees," attacking humans on command. Thanks to the diligence of the military police, the government went on to trumpet, this foreign madman was stopped before he could put his evil drones to work.

And thus was the myth of the killer bee born.

Now, African bees are no more venomous than their European cousins. Neither do they go out of their way to look for targets, human or otherwise. The difference lies in the African bees' defensiveness; when their colonies are attacked or approached, they tend to swarm and sting with abandon, perhaps aware—bees are intelligent creatures, after all—that to do so means death in the defense of their queen. Since their arrival in the Americas, the African purebreds have intermingled with European varieties of honeybee, giving birth to a hybrid, the "Africanized bee." It is these small, graceful creatures that have lately been crossing our border into the American Southwest of late, and giving so many people fits.

To call them "killer bees" is clearly wrong; the more common German bee, appropriately enough, is far more aggressive. And because Western culture, sadly, tends to equate anything African with savagery, "Africanized bees" isn't much help. In Latin America the creatures are called *abejas bravas*, "brave bees," a name unlikely to catch on with any but the savviest gringos. Africanized bees, then, is what we'll have to make do with— with no connotations attached, please, positive or negative.

University of Minnesota professor Marla Spivak is one of the world's leading authorities on Africanized bees, which she has been studying for more than a decade. She smiles at the media accounts of the terror these newcomers portend, but she wants the public to be aware that the bees are no laughing matter, either.

"For the first five to ten years after they appear in a country," Dr. Spivak says, "they cause problems, but only because beekeepers find them hard to work with. When you work a defensive colony you have to become a better beekeeper, really pay attention to what they're doing. Beekeepers can cull out defensive colonies, fortunately, and select only the most gentle characteristics. The problem is really out in the desert. Where you once only had to worry about rattlesnakes and water, you now find Africanized bees, too. They rarely sting unprovoked, but there are a few weirdos out there."

It's always the few weirdos, of course, that get the attention. Even still, although over the last three decades there have been a couple of thousand bee-sting deaths in Latin America—about the same number as in the United States—there have been no recorded unprovoked attacks on the part of Africanized bees.

Indeed, of the forty-one people who died nationwide in 1993 of bee stings, only one was attacked by an Africanized strain. That unfortunate fellow, an eighty-two-year-old man from Río Grande City, Texas, had been stung, an autopsy revealed, about fifty times. "A normally healthy person," Dr. Spivak says, "can take five hundred stings and survive with no problems." But the poor man suffered from a heart condition, and fifty stings were enough to seal his fate.

When a young man was stung to death in Puerto Peñasco, Sonora, on August 19, 1993, Mexican and borderlands newspapers immediately put the blame on "killer bees." (The *abeja brava* has come to earn a bad name south of the border, thanks in some measure to *yanqui* hysteria.) Two weeks later, a sheepish coroner announced that the bees had in fact been Europeans, that the man had been stung only a few times, and that he had died from anaphylactic shock—that is, an allergic reaction.

Dogs and cats have more to worry about than do humans. Naturally curious, they tend to wander around in the dark corners in which bees like to establish colonies: under thick bushes, in trees, in sheds and eaves. On June 5, 1993, a dog in Tucson died after having been stung 150 times; later that month, firefighters in Sasabe, Arizona, removed a swarm after several animals were stung.

There is no way short of keeping animals indoors to rule out absolutely the chances of their being attacked, Dr. Spivak admits. But there is one way to avoid being stung yourself should a swarm decide to share your residence with you: Don't reach for the D-Con. Instead, call a professional beekeeper to come and remove the colony. You will be rid of a potential catastrophe, and the beekeeper will have thirty thousand productive new workers.

The beekeepers could likely use the work, too. Thanks to an agricultural-subsidy program initiated under President Bush and continued under President Clinton, the federal government imports millions of pounds of honey from China each year. China sells this honey for forty cents a pound, a full twenty-five cents less than the basic costs an American producer incurs before market. The result is that native honey is being driven off the market. To fight this, the heads of the largest commercial bee farms in the United States, most of them smack in the middle of South Dakota, want to see Africanized bees brought to the north country. The improved yield may help lower costs and make American honey competitive against Chinese imports, the product of a country with an appalling human-rights record and no modern tradition of industrial quality in any event.

Let Africanized bees do their bit to breed better beekeepers in this country, in other words. Leave them alone, and the news stories will be things of the past.

"You should be concerned," Dr. Spivak concludes. "But not alarmed."

What, then, is all the fuss about?

For whatever reason, people seem to love a good scare. If this were not a well-known truth, Hollywood would not pump out endless Freddy Krueger movies, and the major news media would not fall into a feeding frenzy whenever rain falls on the Midwest or a strong wind rises off the coast of Florida.

And our scares have changed. A century ago, psychiatrist G. Stanley Hall surveyed some 2,000 subjects nationwide about their fears. The leading bugaboo, he found, was lightning and thunder, followed in order by reptiles, strangers and darkness, fire, domestic animals, disease, wild animals, ghosts, and lesser frights.

These fears seem reasonable enough; in the 1890s, after all, America was still a largely rural country, full of lightning strikes and rattlesnakes and prairie fires and rabid skunks. Who knows, maybe it was full of ghosts as well, given our bloody nineteenth century.

Today, nationally, our greatest nightmare involves animals of all kinds, including snakes and insects, followed by the sight of blood, closed spaces, heights, and air travel. Lightning doesn't even figure into the list, although it slays more people annually than bee stings and dog bites combined. Lord knows, however, that given our fondness for gunning each other down, fearing the sight of blood seems perfectly sound.

We have ample industries to fuel our fears: plenty of psycho films, plenty of scare-tactic headline writers and doomsayers, plenty of insurance companies that carefully nurture the image that life can, with the proper policy, be made free of risk.

Apis mellifera scutellata has nested in this panic. It's a creature to be regarded with healthy respect, and at arm's length, viewed from a safe distance as it hives along desert canyon walls and the high branches of mesquite trees.

But let us remember that only six decades have passed since black widows threatened to conquer the earth. That scare seems ridiculous now, and in the years to come, the terror surrounding "killer bees" will seem equally silly. There are plenty of real dangers to worry about instead. More Americans are going to be shot down in drive-by shootings than killed by bees of whatever sort. More Americans will die as a result of drunk drivers, of negligent manufacturers, of cancers caused by soil and groundwater and air pollution. These are all things we can do something about. We would do well to emulate the Africanized bees' industriousness when we finally set to work on them.

The real danger in the rise and spread of the Africanized bee is one of those big-picture issues that come to light only when it's too late to do anything about them. In this case, as Tucson-based scientists Stephen Buchmann and Gary Paul Nabhan report in *Forgotten Pollinators,* that issue is the long-term destruction of native insect populations, especially bees, through the use of agricultural pesticides. New to the region, the Africanized bees have not suffered the same effects, and the relative weakness of long-adapted bee species—which are also suffering from viruses and a particularly ferocious infestation of mites—has opened up a whole new ecological niche for the recent arrivals to exploit. Intensively competitive, the Africanized bees make use of flowering plants before other bees, already weakened, can get to them; the Africanized bees are also not shy about taking over other bees' hives and kidnapping their queens. This, in the long run, will give the newcomers an evolutionary advantage, and it spells doom for the oldtimers.

"The demise of the native bee hardly makes the front page or a spot on the six o'clock news," write Buchmann and Nabhan. "But now the honeybee industry . . . is declining rapidly, too, due to diverse threats—from two mite species, from fungal, bacterial, and viral diseases, and from a host of pesticides [and] herbicides. . . . At the same time, Africanized bees are expanding their occupied range and threaten this vital pollination service"—unless, that is, all the newcomers are tamed and put into the service of the honey industry, which seems an unlikely prospect, given its current state of crisis.

The news is real: once again, the world is being remade around us, brought on by error and ignorance, by misapplied technology and the drive for economic profit at the expense of the natural world. Africanized bees are only a small part of that story, a story of the destruction we have wrought upon ourselves. Only when the natural world begins to fight back will we know how frightened we should really be.

Beetle

"God seems to have an inordinate fondness for beetles," remarked the biologist J.B.S. Haldane, asked to state his view of nature after a long career studying it. Twenty years ago, I recalled his remark while sitting alongside an ancient roadcut in the arid mountains of southern Italy, watching dung beetles at their work. As they made ball bearings of little pieces of cowpie, I thought, yes, wherever you go in the desert, you will find beetles of the most wondrous description, and in numbers that suggest divine favor. Perhaps the same thoughts crossed the mind of the elderly Apache who once unflatteringly compared the Anglo newcomers to his country to carrion beetles, explaining to anthropologist Keith Basso,

> Well, there is this way that carrion beetle reminds us of whitemen—they waste much food. Carrion beetle, when he is young and before he starts to eat meat, just eats a little hole in a leaf and then moves on to eat a little hole in another. He leaves plenty of good food behind him. It is like this with some white people, too. Another way they are the same, these two, is that in the summer they only come out from where they live when it is cool. You only see carrion beetles early in the morning and again in the early evening. It is the same with some white people. In the summer they always want to stay some place where it is cool.

Those invaders are in the desert to stay, but the ancient Greek encyclopedist Aelian assures us, "You will destroy a beetle if you throw roses on it."

It is the scarab beetles of the genus *Amphiocoma,* not the birds and bees, who pollinate the crowfoot buttercups of the Judean Desert, the red flowers beloved of Solomon.

Bighorn sheep

The bighorn sheep, *Ovis canadensis,* is a characteristic animal of the North American deserts. Its range is by no means confined to the dry lands; it can be found throughout the mountains of western North America into Alaska and across into Siberia as far west as the mouth of the Yenesei River. It is the only of the major species of sheep not to have contributed to the standard domesticated varieties, being wild at heart and hard to catch; the modern meadow-shearing sheep instead descend from the moufflon, urial, and argali. The most important domesticated desert-dwelling sheep today, in fact, is the merino, a descendant of Saharan and Arabian desert strains that was once one of Spain's great trade secrets. A voracious variety developed by Roman breeders who grazed them in North Africa until the once-rich coastal grasslands were shorn to the ground, their breeding was subsequently a peninsular royal monopoly until the 1600s, when the Spanish soil could no longer support grazing herbivores in number.

In the late 1980s and early 1990s, scientists working in southwestern Arizona's Cabeza Prieta Mountains built a series of stock tanks to complement the region's natural *tinajas,* or rock cisterns, to capture rainwater. The thinking was that if the availability of water increased, then the area's natural populations of bighorn sheep and pronghorn antelope (*Antilocapra americana*) would also grow. In less than a decade, the famed desert-walker and Cabeza Prieta habitué Bill Broyles reports, water holes increased by a third, and the water available by more than 300

percent. Yet the bighorn and pronghorn populations did not increase, leading biologists to conclude that these animals may not drink water, as such, but rather derive their water from the plant food and even the preternaturally dry air of the desert. (Scientists now worry that the increased water supplies may instead draw more predators to the area, and with them cause an overall decline in the nimble grazers' number.) These animals are also able to hyperconcentrate urine to waste no water when eliminating nitrogenous waste, finely filtering the urine through a structure in the kidney—which all mammals have—called the Loop of Henle, nature's desalinization plant.

Aelian reports the existence of the Libyan *katoblepon*, or creature that looks down, which "is the size of a bull, but it has a more grim expression, for its eyebrows are high and shaggy, and the eyes beneath it are not large like those of oxen, but narrow and bloodshot. . . . It feeds on poisonous roots, and it emits from its throat a pungent and foul-smelling breath, so that the whole air around it is infected, and animals that approach and inhale it are grievously afflicted, lose their voice, and are seized with deathly convulsions. The beast knows its power, and other animals know it as well. They flee as far away from the *katoblepon* as they can." The downward-looking creature was probably a Saharan bighorn, a member of a race of animals now all but extinct in the African desert.

Blowfly

In Aboriginal Australian belief, the blowfly is the psychopomp who conducts souls from this world into the land of the dead, and the blowfly is consequently a figure whose presence is not welcomed in any camp. In Arnhem Land this song is sung:

Ah, the blowfly is whining there, its maggots are eating flesh.
The blowflies buzz, their feet stray over the corpse. . . .
Who is it eating there, whose flesh are they eating?
Ah, my daughter, come back to me!
Ah, our daughter was taken ill. . . .
Ah, my lost, sick child—ah, the blowflies!

This dirge does not suffer in comparison to an odd poem of Emily Dickinson's that, as it happens, features both a fly and death:

I heard a Fly buzz—when I died—
The Stillness in the Room
Was like the Stillness in the Air—
Between the Heaves of Storm

The Eyes around—had wrung them dry—
And Breaths were gathering firm
For that last Onset—when the King
Be witnessed—in the Room—

I willed my Keepsakes—Signed away
What portion of me be
Assignable—and then it was
There interposed a Fly—

With Blue—uncertain stumbling Buzz—
Between the light—and me—
And then the Windows failed—and then
I could not see to see

If you should see a blowfly in the Australian desert, then, or
perhaps even in a drawing room in New England, the best strat-
egy, useless though it will ultimately be, is to turn and walk away.

Butterfly

Remember that the most beautiful things in
the world are the most useless: peacocks and
lilies, for instance.

John Ruskin

Language is fossil poetry, and fossil history. "There are words
like *moon* and *labor*," writes the poet Thomas McGrath,
"which, if we look inside, contain more rings of growth than
even the oldest tree."

I have long entertained a theory that the word for *butterfly* is
likely to be euphonious in any language that has a term for it,
and so I have made it a habit to ask native speakers if their word
is thought to be pretty in their idiom. This tiny sampling of the
world's four thousand living languages turns up some beautiful
words indeed:

Acoma	*buh'rai*
Arabic	*farasha*
Dutch	*vlinder*
German	*Schmetterling*
Greek	*petalou'da*
Hebrew	*parpar*
Hungarian	*lepke*
Italian	*farfalla*
Japanese	*chou*
Kyaka Enga	*maemae*
Latin	*papilio*
Lushootseed	*yubec*
Maltese	*farfetta*
Nahuatl	*papalotl*
Ndumba	*kaapura'rora*
Osage	*dsithato'ga*
Polish	*motyl*
Portuguese	*borboleta*
Romanian	*fluture*
Russian	*babochka*
Spanish	*mariposa*
Swahili	*kipepeo*
Tohono O'odham	*hohokimal*
Turkish	*kelebek*
Yaqui	*vaisevo'i*

Butterfly is not only beautiful, but he also inhabits beautiful places and signals beautiful things to come—such as rain, always a wonder in the desert. Yaqui deer singers honor that instance:

Over there, I, where the flower-covered
 sun comes out
  they are emerging
   all through the wilderness world
    in a row they are flying

White butterflies, they say,
In a row are flying.

In O'odham legend Butterfly once married a human woman
and settled at a place called Vapik-oiduk, meaning land with a
near-underground water supply. The moist earth produced an
abundance of crops, commemorated in this song:

Butterfly has a farm
Which is in a sacred place.
In that farm grows the corn
And there is too much work
For a woman.

Owing to all that work, the human woman left Butterfly, who
now lives alone. She, the O'odham say, went on to teach other
women wicked ways.

Camel

The camel, as the old bon mot has it, is a horse designed by committee: an ungainly creature, it is the largest of the ruminants, the creatures that, alone of all mammals, arise from the ground hind legs first. If you have ever been spat on by one you know what it is like to have been visited by demons. Its foul spittle, however, is probably not why the camel is considered unclean by the strictures of Leviticus, but instead because it was the steed of the Bedouin enemy, and thus an enemy to city people and cultivators.

The camel is one of the earliest mammals to have been domesticated—even today, humans have tamed only a few of the mammal species offering themselves to the task—and one of the few to have been domesticated first by nonagricultural desert societies. We associate the camel with the North African desert, but it is a fairly recent importation there from the deserts of Persia, brought into the Sahara as a beast of burden in Roman times at about the time the last native elephants died off, the Romans having killed them to supply ivory to the empire.

Now, deserts are windy places, windy because they abound in solar energy, the driving force of the world's supply of moving air. One wind, the *simoun* (from the Arabic word for poison), shrieks over the Sahara, whipping up sand and dust into fearful, sharp-grained *chevaux de frise*. Herodotus, the great Greek traveler and historian, whom his younger contemporary Thucydides uncharitably called "the father of lies," doubtless got it right when he reported the story of a Libyan army that marched off two and a half millennia ago into the deep Sahara to find and subdue the lord of these storms. The expedition never returned, "disappearing, in battle array, with drums and cymbals beating, into a red cloud of swirling sand." The Assyrians, it is said, did much the same, sending squads of archers to combat the approaching clouds. And for good reason: a duststorm once buried Ur of the Chaldees, cause enough to seek vengeance.

The *simoun* has many local equivalents: the Moroccan *sirocco*, the Libyan *ghibli*, the Saudi *khamsin*, the Egyptian *zoboa*, the Australian "brickfielder," the Mongolian *karaburan*, the Sudanese *haboob*, the Mauritanian *harmattan*, and the Indian *loo*, which Rudyard Kipling describes in his story "The Man Who Would Be King" as a "red-hot wind from the westward, booming among the tinder-dry trees and pretending that the rain was on its heels." The logic of those winds seems to have prompted evolution to make a few alterations in the master plan; recently, biologists have concluded that camels, strange creatures to begin with, evolved so that, standing, they can clear the sand-laden zone of air, which goes up only to about six feet, slightly lower than the average camel's height. Other creatures, such as the antelope-like saiga of Central Asia and certain kinds of desert hares, have filtering tissues surrounding their respiratory tracts that give them the same adaptive advantage.

Nikolai Prejevalsky, the Russian scientist and explorer who crossed the high deserts of Central Asia atop a string of Bactrian camels, came to have a great respect for his steeds:

> During the excessive heats in summer, the camels are attracted by the cool temperature of the higher valleys of Altyn-tagh, and make their way thither to an altitude of 11,000 feet, and even higher, for our guides informed us that they are occasionally found on the lofty plateau on its southern side. Here the chief attraction for them are the springs of water, to say nothing of the greater abundance of camel's thorn (*calidium*), and their favourite, but less plentiful *Hedysarum*. In winter the wild camel keeps

entirely to the lower and warmer desert, only entering the mountains from time to time.

Unlike the domesticated animal, whose chief characteristics are cowardice, stupidity, and apathy, the wild variety is remarkable for its sagacity and admirably developed senses. Its sight is marvellously keen, hearing exceedingly acute, and sense of smell wonderfully perfect. The hunters told us that a camel could scent a man several versts off, see him, however cautiously he might approach, from a great distance, and hear the slightest rustle of his footsteps. Once aware of its danger, it instantly takes flight, and never stops for some dozens, or even hundreds of versts. A camel I fired at certainly ran twenty versts without stopping, as I saw by its traces, and probably farther still, had I been able to follow it, for it turned into a ravine off our line of march. One would suppose that so uncouth an animal would be incapable of climbing mountains; the contrary, however, is actually the case, for we often saw the tracks and droppings of camels in the narrowest gorges, and on slopes steep enough to baffle the hunter. Here their footprints are mingled with those of the mountain sheep (*Pseudo nahoor*) and the arkari (*Ovis poli*). So incredible did this appear, that we could hardly believe our eyes when we saw it. The wild camel is very swift, its pace being almost invariably a trot. In this respect, however, the domesticated species will, in a long distance, overtake a good galloper. It is very weak when wounded, and drops directly if it is hit by a bullet of small calibre, such as the hunters of Lob-nor use.

We were unable to learn the duration of a camel's life; some are known to live to a great age.

Aelian observes that the camels of the Caspii, the eponymous people of the Caspian Sea region, which Prejevalsky crossed, were innumerable, "and the largest are the size of the largest horses and have beautiful hair. . . . Accordingly their priests and the wealthiest and most powerful of the Caspii clothe themselves in garments made from the camels' hair." Herodotus rejoins that camels have four thighbones in their hind legs, and that their genitals face backwards. He was also shocked to report that while camels would never dream of copulating openly, their Massagetae drivers did, an affront to the camels'— and Herodotus's—natural sense of decency.

Although it has long been popularly supposed that the camel's back is curved, its backbone is as straight as that of a horse; its hump is composed of not bone but fat, and a malnourished or overworked camel will often not have a hump at all. The one-humped dromedary (*Camelus dromedarius*) of the Saharan and Arabian deserts and the two-humped Bactrian camel (*Camelus bactrianus*) differ largely in that the latter has shorter limb-bones than the former; the dromedary, too, has a vestigial anterior hump that seems to have shrunk from the Bactrian's pronounced two humps in response to drier conditions. That reserve of fat enables the camel to store water and reabsorb it on long desert voyages when food and water are scarce, leading to the supposition that camels can travel for months at a time without taking a drink.

Adelard of Bath, an English theologian, spent several years in Syria and reported the things he had learned in his *Quæstiones Naturales,* written in about 1117 but not published until 1480. Among the other learning he delivers to his foil, a young nephew, is a description of the camel and other ruminants. Adelard remarks, "It is a little difficult for you and me to argue about animals. I, with Reason for my guide, have learned one thing from my Arab teachers, you, something different; dazzled by the outward show of authority you wear a head-stall. For what else should we call authority but a head-stall?" When his nephew asks why some animals chew cud, Adelard replies,

> The natures of animals, like those of human beings, differ. Some of them are naturally hot, others cold, some moist, and others dry.

Those which are hot more readily digest the food they have taken in, and more easily change it into blood, while cold animals have more difficulty with this. Everything subject to change is altered more easily by heat than by cold, for fire has, as it were, the property of sundering what is conjoined. Consequently, those animals which have a hot stomach easily digest their food. Others, however, which are of a cold nature, being unable to digest their food, bring it back, and use their teeth again upon it, in order that by a second process it may the more readily be softened: this is done by oxen, goats, and similar animals, whom the Greek physicists call "melancholic." How all these animals are of a cold nature is clear enough to the physicists, and you may get an idea of it as follows: it is for this reason, that they have both their fat harder, and what is commonly called the paunch more solid; while others, as being warmer, have the fat softer, it being better digested, or to use the common phrase, more greasy.

Why camels should have cold natures we do not learn, but the ancients also supposed that the camel dislikes clear water, preferring to drink muddy, dirty water over any other. Modern science does not bear up this observation, although camels do tend to step in whatever body of water they happen to be drinking from, thus stirring up mud and silt from the bed. With clumsiness comes a reputation for obstinacy, as an Egyptian proverb tells: "The camel curses its parents when it has to go up a hill, and its Maker when it has to go down."

Seeking elusive first causes, a medieval German philosopher-naturalist once supposed that the production of butter from churning cow's milk came by way of suggestion from Arab traders to the West. These traders, he wrote, manufactured butter by heaving canteens full of camel milk across the saddle, and then ate the congealed contents at the end of a long desert passage.

Camels have been put to other uses in the kitchen as well. The Australian explorer Peter Egerton Warburton (1813–1889) crossed the continent with a string of camels, which began to die from eating poisonous plants or from the heat, whereupon Warburton and his human companions began to eat their unfortunate transport. "No shred was passed over," Warburton recalled. "Head, feet, hide, tail, all went into the boiling pot. . . . The tough, thick hide was cut up and parboiled. The coarse hair was then scraped off with a knife and the leatherlike substance replaced in the pot and stewed until it became like the inside of a carpenter's glue pot, both to the taste and to the smell."

Coatimundi

In the desert
I saw a creature, naked, bestial,
Who squatting upon the ground,
Held his heart in his hands,
And ate of it.
I said, "Is it good, friend?"
"It is bitter—bitter," he answered;
"But I like it
Because it is bitter,
And because it is my heart."

Just what kind of creature Stephen Crane, the author of this strange poem, encountered in that desert we will never know. If it was a coatimundi (*Nasua nasua*), it would have been eating something other than its heart: likelier the heart of a cow, an offering that drew the raccoon-like coatimundi from its Sierra Madrean woodland home down to the desert floor for an easy feast.

The story is this: in the 1880s, with the end of the Apache Indian wars, cattle by the hundreds of thousands were driven into the arid grasslands of western New Mexico and eastern Arizona. The effect on the landscape was devastating. Huge herds roamed across the range, devouring nearly every plant in their path, shunning only the prickly pear and poisonous lupines. The paths that the herds cut into the fragile ground opened up with constant use and rainstorms to form great arroyos, or ravines, that diverted water from natural courses. Within the space of a few years the formerly lush grasslands had been gnawed to the ground by herds of introduced Jersey, Guernsey, Charolais, and longhorn cattle. The man who introduced longhorns to the Southwest, a forester and former Apache fighter named Will Barnes, later confessed in his memoirs, "We fondly imagined that these wonderful ranges would last forever and couldn't be overstocked." Another rancher, C. H. Bayless, who ran herds along the middle San Pedro River, echoed Barnes: "Vegetation does not thrive as it once did . . . because the seed is gone, the roots are gone, and the soil is gone. This is all the direct result of over-stocking and cannot be prevented on open range where the land is not subject to private control."

Cattle and the pecuniary promise they brought changed the tenor of the West as well. The Indian nations had truly been subdued—in General Phil Sheridan's words, so that the West could "be covered with speckled cattle and the festive cowboy." But the conflicting interests of miners, ranchers, farmers, and townspeople quickly erased the hope of peace. Large ranches like the Aztec Land and Cattle Company of northern Arizona, with a spread of more than a million acres, took to hiring cow-boys who were more proficient with guns than branding irons, and a range war soon erupted across the Southwest. The Aztec's cowboys terrorized Mormon settlers along the Mogollon Rim, yielding the few ghost towns to exist in the Kingdom of the Latter-Day Saints. Rival cattle companies waged war against each other. Towns of the Southwest became charnel houses in which, as Apache fighter John Cremony observed, "men walked the streets with double-barreled shotguns and hunted each other as sportsmen hunt for game." The time was so vio-lent at home and abroad that Mark Twain proposed changing the stars in the American flag to skulls and crossbones.

Small farmers, too, fell victim to ranching enterprises, for the ranchers required ready access to water for their herds, water that now flowed in acequías to the small fields of corn and wheat that dotted the Southwest's river valleys. Some farmers were more than glad to sell out, but others had to be persuaded by force. The obituary columns of newspapers like the *Tombstone Telegraph* and *Silver City Independent* mushroomed as the ranching inter-ests, in Bernard De Voto's words, "did their utmost to keep the nester—the farmer, the actual settler, the man who could create local and permanent wealth—out of the West and to terrorize or bankrupt him where he could not be kept out."

Nature has always provided the deserts with defense mechanisms against the vanity of human wishes, however. Apart from the occasional simoon and cyclical flood, the most powerful has been drought, and drought was what nature visited upon the Southwest in 1892. O'odham shamans had foretold the disaster two decades earlier, when a massive earthquake in Sonora rumbled throughout the Papaguería, with aftershocks lasting ten seconds and more; they prophesied that I'itoi, the creator, was about to change the face of the earth. Finding in the earthquake a convenient excuse, cattlemen would later claim that it indeed produced the great drought of the 1890s.

The drought settled in for a full decade. The year 1892 was perhaps the worst; out of the already denuded landscape no new grasses sprang forth, and unacclimated English breeds like Devons and Alderneys quickly fell prey to exhaustion, hunger, and thirst. Within a year the hardier Sonoran and Texan cattle joined them, and, as a rancher later reminisced, a person could "actually throw a rock from one carcass to another" across the length of southern New Mexico and Arizona. The rancher did not exaggerate; within three years some two million cattle had died, more than half of the aggregate herds. Men and women died, too, and cowboys were reduced to straining what little water they could find through cheesecloth and burlap in order to filter out the one creature that thrived at the time, the maggots that sprang from rotting corpses.

With the dead cattle came the coatimundi, a strange example of an ecological colonization brought on by the harshest disaster.

Coyote

"For all the toll the desert takes it gives compensations, deep breaths, deep sleep, and the communion of stars," writes Mary Austin in her famous book *The Land of Little Rain.* "Of no account you who lie out there watching, nor the lean coyote that stands off in the scrub from you and howls and howls." To which Shelley Starr, whose son Bill's terrier was attacked by coyotes outside Tucson in January 1996, supplies this rejoinder: "They don't care who you are. If you're near them and they're well-fed, they just walk by you. They're not afraid of you. They're sort of arrogant."

Mark Twain, in *Roughing It*, captures the sometime glories and sometime arrogance of *Canis latrans*:

> Along about an hour after breakfast we saw the first prairie-dog villages, the first antelope, and the first wolf. If I remember rightly, this latter was the regular *cayote* (pronounced ky-o-te) of the farther deserts. And if it was, he was not a pretty creature or respectable either, for I got well acquainted with his race afterward, and can speak with confidence. The cayote is a long, skinny, sick and sorry-looking skeleton, with a gray wolf-skin stretched over it, a tolerably bushy tail that forever sags down with a despairing expression of forsakenness and misery, a furtive and evil eye, and a long, sharp face, with slightly lifted lip and exposed teeth. He has a general slinking expression all over. The cayote is a living, breathing allegory of Want. He is *always* hungry. He is always poor, out of luck and friendless. The meanest creatures despise him, and even the fleas would desert him for a velocipede. He is so spiritless and cowardly that even while his exposed teeth are pretending a threat, the rest of his face is apologizing for it. And he is so homely!—so scrawny, and ribby, and coarse-haired, and pitiful. When he sees you he lifts his lip and lets a flash of his teeth out, and then turns a little out of the course

he was pursuing, depresses his head a bit, and strikes a long, soft-footed trot through the sagebrush, glancing over his shoulder at you, from time to time, till he is about out of easy pistol range, and then he stops and takes a deliberate survey of you; he will trot fifty yards and stop again—another fifty and stop again; and finally the gray of his gliding body blends with the gray of the sage-brush, and he disappears. All this is when you make no demonstration against him; but if you do, he develops a livelier interest in his journey, and instantly electrifies his heels and puts such a deal of real estate between himself and your weapon, that by the time you have raised the hammer you see that you need a Minié rifle, and by the time you have got him in line you need a rifled cannon, and by the time you have drawn a bead on him you see well enough that nothing but an unusually long-winded streak of lightning could reach him where he is now. But if you start a swift-footed dog after him, you will enjoy it ever so much—especially if it is a dog that has a good opinion of himself, and has been brought up to think he knows something about speed. The cayote will go swinging gently off on that deceitful trot of his, and every little while he will smile a fraudful smile over his shoulder that will fill that dog entirely full of encouragement and worldly ambition, and make him lay his head still lower to the ground, and stretch his neck further to the front, and pant more fiercely, and stick his tail out straighter behind, and move his furious legs with a yet wilder frenzy, and leave a broader and broader, and higher and denser cloud of desert sand smoking behind, and marking his long wake across the level plain! And all this time the dog is only a short twenty feet behind the cayote, and to save the soul of him he cannot understand why it is that he cannot get perceptibly closer; and he begins to get aggravated, and it makes him madder and madder to see how gently the cayote glides along and never pants or sweats or ceases to smile; and he grows still more and more incensed to see how shamefully he has been taken in by an entire stranger, and what an ignoble swindle that long, calm, soft-footed trot is; and next he notices that he is getting fagged, and that the cayote actually has to slacken speed a little to keep from running away from him—and then that town-dog is mad in earnest, and he begins to strain and weep and swear, and paw the sand higher than ever, and reach for the cayote with concentrated and desperate energy. This "spurt" finds him six feet behind the gliding enemy, and two miles from his friends. And then, in the instant that a wild new hope is lighting up his face, the cayote turns and smiles blandly upon him once more, and with a something about it which seems to say: "Well, I shall have to tear myself away from you, bub—business is business, and it will not do for me to be fooling along this way all day"—and forthwith there is a rushing sound, and the sudden splitting of a long crack through the atmosphere, and behold that dog is solitary and alone in the midst of a vast solitude!

It makes his head swim. He stops, and looks all around; climbs the nearest sand-mound, and gazes into the distance; shakes his head reflectively, and then, without a word, he turns and jogs along back to his train, and takes up a humble position under the hindmost wagon, and feels unspeakably mean, and looks ashamed, and hangs his tail at half-mast for a week. And for as much as a year after that, whenever there is a great hue and cry after a cayote, that dog will merely glance in that direction without emotion, and apparently observe to himself, "I believe I do not wish any of the pie."

The cayote lives chiefly in the most desolate and forbidding deserts, along with the lizard, the jackass rabbit and the raven, and gets an uncertain and precarious living, and earns it. He seems to subsist almost wholly on the carcasses of oxen, mules and horses that have dropped out of emigrant trains and died, and upon windfalls of carrion, and occasional legacies of offal bequeathed to him by white men who have been opulent enough to have something better to butcher than condemned army bacon. He will eat anything in the world that his first cousins, the desert-frequenting tribes of Indians will, and they will eat anything they can bite. It is a curious fact that these latter are the only creatures known to history who will eat nitroglycerine and ask for more if they survive.

The cayote of the deserts beyond the Rocky Mountains has a peculiarly hard time of it, owing to the fact that his relations, the Indians, are just as apt to be the first to detect a seductive scent on the desert breeze, and follow the fragrance to the late ox it emanated from, as he is himself; and when this occurs he has to content himself with sitting off at a little distance watching those people strip off and dig out everything edible, and walk off with it. Then he and the waiting ravens explore the skeleton and polish the bones. It is considered that the cayote, and the obscene bird, and the Indian of the desert, testify their blood kinship with each other in that they live together in the waste places of the earth on terms of perfect confidence and friendship, while hating all other creatures and yearning to assist at their funerals. He does not mind going a hundred miles to breakfast, and a hundred and fifty to dinner, because he is sure to have three or four days between meals, and he can just as well be traveling and looking at the scenery as lying around doing nothing and adding to the burdens of his parents.

We soon learned to recognize the sharp, vicious bark of the cayote as it came across the murky plain at night to disturb our dreams among the mail-sacks; and remembering his forlorn aspect and his hard fortune, made shift to wish him the blessed novelty of a long day's good luck and a limitless larder the morrow.

The Navajo tell this story about the character they call Prairie Wolf:

Once Prairie Wolf went out hunting with his father-in-law, and they rested at night on the top of a rugged mountain where they lit their camp-fire and cooked some meat for supper. As they were lying down to sleep Prairie Wolf said, "This hill is called the Hill of the Burned Moccasins." The old man had never heard this extraordinary name before, and he could not help wondering at it until the Wind God whispered in his ear, "Change your moccasins." Before he fell asleep he took Prairie Wolf's moccasins and put them under his head, and he put his moccasins in place of Prairie Wolf's. Late in the night Prairie Wolf rose softly, took the moccasins from under the old man's head, and buried them in the hot embers. When they woke in the morning, the old man pretended to look in vain for his lost moccasins.

"Ah!" said Prairie Wolf, "You forgot that this is the Hill of the Burned Moccasins."

"Oh! there they are under your head," said the elder. "Thank you for taking such good care of them."

"Yes," said Prairie Wolf, "I have taken care of them for you; but the ground is so nice and soft on this mountain that I'll go barefoot today."

Coyote, known as Ban to the Tohono O'odham, figures as a Trickster character in the mythologies of many western Native American peoples. This just-so story recounts one of Coyote's more remarkable accomplishments:

It is said that there are three dwellings—above us, here on earth, and below us.

Eagle lived up there above us. One day he became angry because Coyote was always so noisy. He came down saying he was going to take Coyote's wife away from him. "Then what will Coyote say?" So Eagle came down.

When he arrived, Coyote had gone hunting. He hadn't killed anything and was still out wandering around, so he didn't see Eagle take his wife. Later, he couldn't find her and went out looking for her. He got hungry, found a carcass, and began to eat it.

Then Buzzard came and said, "I know where your wife is. I'll tell you where she is and take you there. But from now on, whenever you kill something, you must always leave something for me."

Coyote promised to do as Buzzard said.

They ate. Then Buzzard said, "Sit on my back and we'll fly up to the heavens. But don't turn around or you'll fall off."

"I won't," Coyote said.

So they went up and up, far away from the earth.

Coyote thought, "Maybe I'll never see my home again. I'll look just one time." He looked back and fell. Buzzard turned around and tried to catch him. When they were very near earth Buzzard finally got Coyote.

Buzzard said, "I tell you, don't turn around, and we'll be able to get safely up to the heavens."

Coyote assured him that he wouldn't, but he was so homesick that every time they went up he looked back and fell off Buzzard. This happened four times.

Then Buzzard glued his eyes shut with mesquite pitch, and they finally got up to the heavens. He unplastered Coyote's eyes and said, "Go over there and see your wife. Tell me when you do, and we'll take her back from Eagle. But don't get caught. If you do Eagle will kill you."

Coyote nodded and went off. He had only gone a little way when he started to get hungry. He thought, "Maybe someone will give me some food." He stood in front of someone's ramada and said, "Hey, you have a visitor."

Someone inside said, "Don't feed him. He lives far below us. Whenever I go down there and get hungry they chase me away from their fields."

Coyote left. He went to someone else's house and said, "You have a visitor."

Someone inside said, "Don't feed him. He lives far below us. Whenever I go down there to catch animals they chase me away."

Coyote left again. He began to think he was going to die of hunger. Then he decided to steal something. He went to a house where no one was home and found a sack of cornmeal.

He was about to eat when someone yelled at him, "Scat! Scat!"

Coyote ran away with the sack in his teeth. The cornmeal that Coyote scattered when he ran away can be seen up there now, in the sky.

Chuck Jones, the greatest *Canis latrans* mythmaker of our time, offers that there are only a few rules that Coyote can be made to obey—at least, that is, in the famed cartoons Jones crafted:

1. The Road Runner cannot harm the Coyote except by going "Beep-Beep!"
2. No outside force can harm the Coyote—only his own ineptitude or the failure of Acme products.
3. The Coyote could stop anytime—If he were not a fanatic. ("A fanatic is one who redoubles his effort when he has forgotten his aim." —George Santayana)
4. No dialogue ever, except "Beep-Beep!"
5. The Road Runner must stay on the road—otherwise, logically he would not be called Road Runner.
6. All Action must be confined to the natural environment of the two characters—the southwest American desert.
7. All materials, tools, weapons, or mechanical conveniences must be obtained from the Acme Corporation.
8. Whenever possible, make gravity the Coyote's greatest enemy.
9. The Coyote is always more humiliated than harmed by his failures.

And thus humiliated, as Mark Twain said, Coyote slinks away to fight the odds another day.

Desert tortoise

Aelian tells us that "tortoises are a product of Libya; they have a most cruel look, and they live in the mountains, and their shell is good for making lyres." Elsewhere in his *On the Characteristics of Animals,* he adds, "the land-tortoise is a most lustful creature, at least the male is; the female mates unwillingly. . . . The female couples only when facing the male, and when he has satisfied himself he leaves, and the female is unable to right herself because of the weight of her shell and the fact that she has been pressed into the ground by the male's weight. She is abandoned to provide a meal for other animals, especially eagles." Female tortoises were understandably reluctant to mate, Aelian continues, but the males know

how to cast a spell on them with the use of some mysterious desert herb; this makes the females crazy with desire to mate without any concern for their future.

Theophrastus says that the desert tortoise, after eating marjoram, "treats vipers with contempt. But if it lacks marjoram it arms against its enemy by eating rue. If it fails to find either, it is slaughtered."

Dingo

The much-maligned dingo (*Canis dingo*) is in some ways, like the Gila monster (*q.v.*), a living fossil. Osteologically, it retains very ancient elements, as does its cousin the pariah dog (*Canis indicus*) of the Indian subcontinent, and it roams the earth at the same time as does the inimical descendant of one of its ancestral branches—the sheepdog.

The dingo came across the land bridge from Indochina with its domesticators, the Melanesian aborigines who colonized Australia in the Dreamtime, some fifty thousand years ago. From there it fanned out, living sometimes wild, sometimes alongside humans, across the continent.

The Aranda have this story about ravenous Dingo:

> Chicken Hawk, Hawk, and Dingo were camping together on a mountainside in Maranunnga country. Dingo went out and gathered yams. Returning to camp, he said, "Brothers, let's take a special stick and make fire so that we can cook this food." But Dingo kept breaking the sticks he was twirling to make fire. So he said, "I'm going to go find a fire stick and make a good fire."
>
> He went out and hid behind a pandanus tree. Women had been collecting yams and other food, and they came back to camp with them. They made a fire. When the wood had burned down they

brushed off the ashes and exposed the burning coals. Dingo jumped up to steal a fire stick, but the women saw him and chased him off. He returned to his camp and said, "Brothers, I'm too big. The women saw me and chased me away." But Chicken Hawk and Hawk said, "You try again." He went back and tried again to steal away fire, but the women chased him. He returned to camp and said, "It's no good. They see me and drive me from their fire. My hands are sore from twirling sticks. You go, Chicken Hawk."

So Chicken Hawk went and hid behind the pandanus tree. The women made their fire and kept a lookout for Dingo. Chicken Hawk remained there unnoticed. Then he swooped down and stole a piece of glowing wood, screaming, "Diiid! Diiid!" The women ran after him, but he got away. As he flew off, he dropped little pieces of charcoal that you can see from Birangma to Djungarabaja Hill.

Back at his camp he found Dingo, who had grown impatient and eaten the yams raw. "Ah!" cried Chicken Hawk. "Here I brought fire, but you ate them raw!" That is why Dingo doesn't talk, as birds do, and why he bolts down his food raw; he just couldn't wait to eat. But the three still wait there at Djungarabaja, dreaming.

Always hungry, the dingo harried the flocks and herds of the European conquerors of Australia, incidentally holding the populations of other introduced species, such as the rabbit, in check. Because of its fondness for livestock the dingo was targeted as an enemy of agricultural civilization, and it was massacred by the hundreds of thousands, a destruction that continues even today. Now, as told by this Associated Press story of August 2, 1995, even the dingo, that master of resilience if not of his own impatience, is fast disappearing from this chewed-up world:

SYDNEY—The dingo, Australia's wild native dog and a feature of the outback for 4,000 years, is sliding toward extinction, a scientist said.

The dingo, a close relative of the wolf, is being absorbed into the domestic dog population and will breed itself out of existence within 50 to 100 years, research scientist Laurie Corbett told Reuters.

"The dingo's gene pool is being swamped. It will be hybridized into oblivion because of breeding with dogs," said Corbett, of the government's Commonwealth Science and Industry Research Association.

Eagle

The acrobatics of the golden eagle, *Aquila chrysaetos,* long anointed the king of the birds, have impressed observers at least from Homeric times; the *Iliad* and *Odyssey* are shot through with references to this majestic hunter. Distributed evenly across the northern hemisphere, the species is familiar in the North American desert, where it can be seen in numbers in the winter and spring. *Aquila chrysaetos* makes for a marvelous sight, as the ornithologist William Brewster noted in 1911 when he recorded a golden eagle swooping down on a great blue heron over the northern Mexican desert:

> Drifting, presently, over the place where the Heron had settled and evidently noticing the big bird for the first time, the Eagle checked his flight in the middle of a half-completed circle to poise for an instant on rapidly vibrating wings, precisely as a Kingfisher will hover over a school of minnows. Then he swooped, apparently as straight and vertically as a heavy stone may fall, yet all the time revolving like a spinning rifle bullet, if more slowly, thereby showing us his (normally) upper and under parts alternately and making no less than four or five such turns before passing out of sight. Never before have I seen anything of the kind that seemed nearly so wonderful and impressive. As the great bird plunged headlong, from a height of at least one hundred yards, his wings, apparently set and almost closed, made a sound like that of a strong wind blowing through pine branches. His momentum must have been tremendous as he neared the earth. How it was finally checked and what else transpired behind

the line of fallen trees I am, of course, quite unable to report. Without doubt the Eagle swooped at the Heron and quite as certainly failed to strike it down; for after an outburst of loud and prolonged squawking it rose above the trees and flew off at its very best pace, evidently badly frightened. Perhaps the Eagle had merely been amusing itself by bullying it, a diversion to which all strong-willed birds of prey are more or less inclined.

But eagles, while striking fear and awe, have also taken much undeserved bad press. For one thing, an early observer said that the eagle's nest "stinks most offensively." Another noted, the eagle is "an excellent artist at stealing young pigs, which prey he carries alive to his nest, at which time the poor pig makes such a noise overhead that strangers have thought there were flying sows and pigs in that country." Flying pigs seem to have diminished in number in recent years in the deserts of the world, perhaps as eagle populations have fallen. The idea that the nest and even the bird itself are possessed of foul odors continues nonetheless, although one careful student, Russell M. Kempton, remarked, "no offensive odors were noted during five years of observation (except when the nestlings would regurgitate for me)."

In some desert cultures of North America the eagle represents death (and, sometimes, the transformation of the worthy human soul into a bird). For that reason, some anthropologists conjecture, historical Chumash and Diegueño traditions, since lost, included the sacrifice of an eagle (or, rarely, a condor) at the winter solstice, when the year is at its shortest and the sun closest to its death, in an effort to stave off their own demise.

Death is the constant companion of the desert nomads of Central Asia, who endure spectacular hardships in their peregrinations. The protagonist of Andrei Platonov's story "Dzhan," Nazar Chagatayev, has been charged with bringing socialism to the people of Turkmenistan, but he finds that the eagles of the sand have other plans for him:

Nazar half-opened his eyes: just beyond his feet two enormous birds were walking, moving away toward a sand dune opposite him. Chagatayev had never seen such birds; they looked like the eagle-carrion vultures of the steppes and at the same time like wild, dark swans. Their beaks were like vultures' beaks, but their thick, powerful necks were longer than those of eagles, and their solid legs carried high the delicate, airy bodies of true swans. The strong wings of one bird were a pure gray in color, while the other had blue, red, and gray feathers. This one was probably the female. Both birds seemed to have on trousers of snowy-white down. Even from one side, Chagatayev noticed little black spots on the female; these were fleas digging through the down into the stomach of the bird. Both birds looked like enormous nestlings which were not yet used to being alive, and were moving with extreme care.

The day had grown hot and dreary, little sandstorms were whirling across the surface of the sand, evening still stood high in the sky, above the light and the warmth. The two birds walked onto the sand dune opposite Chagatayev and looked at him with their thoughtful, farseeing eyes. Chagatayev watched the birds from under his half-closed eyelids, and he could see even the gray, thin color of their eyes as they looked at him full of thought and of attention. The female was cleaning the talons of its feet with its beak, and spitting out of its mouth some kind of old leavings, perhaps a remnant of the clawed-up Nazar-Shakir. The male rose into the air, but the female stayed where it was. The enormous bird flew low to one side, then soared upward with several flappings of its wings, and almost at once began to fall straight toward him. Chagatayev felt the wind in his face before the bird hit him. He could see its white, clean breast in front of his face, and its gray, clear eyes, not wicked but thoughtful, because the bird had now noticed that the man was alive, and watching it. Chagatayev lifted his revolver, held it with both hands, and fired straight at the head of the bird dropping down upon him. In the white down of the bird's breast, blown out by the speed of its downward flight, a dark spot appeared, and then the wind blew all the down and wisps of feathers around the spot of the direct hit, and for a moment the body of the eagle held itself motionless in the air above him.

The bird closed its gray eyes, and then they opened by themselves, but they no longer saw anything—the bird was dead. It lay across Chagatayev's body in the same position in which it had been falling, its breast against the man's breast, its head on his head, burying its beak in Chagatayev's thick hair, spreading wide its black, helpless wings on both sides of him, with its feathers and down strewed all over Chagatayev. Chagatayev himself fainted from the force of the blow, but he was not wounded; the bird had simply stunned him since the dangerous speed of its fall had been braked by the bullet. Chagatayev started up with sharp pain: the second bird, the female, had driven its beak into his right leg and having pulled out some of his flesh was flying off into the air. Chagatayev, holding the revolver with both hands again, fired twice but missed; the gigantic bird disappeared behind the sand dunes, and then he saw it flying away at a great height.

Other desert peoples had a different view of the eagle, finding in it something other than a harbinger and bringer of death. A Mojave singer of the Ghost Dance saw in the eagle the possibility of rebirth:

> *I circle around, I circle around*
>
> *The boundaries of the earth*
> *The boundaries of the earth*
>
> *Wearing the long wing feathers as I fly*
> *Wearing the long wing feathers as I fly*

And the Tingarri of Australia invoke the eagle as a spirit that will help bring rain; if the eagle brings rain, and if the Tingarri build their houses to resemble an eagle's nest, the thinking goes, then rain will come to the desert:

Forked stick and rafters, floor posts
with a roof like an eagle's nest
lie by a billabong where goose eggs
give the water its huge expanse.

My people build, thinking of rain—
rain and wind from the west, clouds
slowly spreading over the billabong—
while we raise our grass huts.

Our chests heave like clouds
as we call out for the rain to fall.
Rain! dampen us with your deluge
as soon as we build our shelters.

For their part, the O'odham tell of a young man who transformed himself into an eagle. The people took this as a portent of disaster and tried to kill the unfortunate shapeshifter. The man-eagle left the desert and flew up high into the wild mountains, the country of the Apache enemy, where he lived by killing the ever-abundant deer, so many that the people grew hungry. They waged war on the man-eagle, and he on them, for generations, until he racked up a considerably greater body count than the first O'odham. Then, to top it off, the man-eagle took some of the dead Indians and turned them into whites, who did not understand the language of the O'odham, who even signaled "yes" and "no" differently, and who continued to wage the war that the man-eagle had begun in first time.

Eland

The Bushman creation story features elands as the first creatures, along with humankind, in the world:

> Cagn's wife, Coti, took her husband's knife and used it to sharpen a digging stick, and she dug roots to eat. When Cagn found that she had spoiled his knife, he scolded her and said evil things should come to her. Upon this she conceived and brought forth a little eland's calf in the fields, and she told her husband, and she said she did not know what sort of a child it was, and he went to see it, and told Coti to grind *canna* [magical herbs] so that he might inquire what it was. She did so, and he went and sprinkled those charms on the animal, and asked it, "Are you this animal? Are you that animal?" but it remained silent till he asked it, "Are you an eland (Tsha)?", when it said "Aaaa."
>
> Then he took it and folded it in his arms, and went and got a gourd, in which he put it, and took it to a secluded kloof [cliff] enclosed by hills and precipices, and left it to grow there. He was at that time making all animals and things, and making them fit for the use of men, and making snares and weapons. He made then the partridge and the striped mouse, and he made the wind in order that the game should smell up the wind, —so they run up the wind still. Cagn took three sticks and sharpened them, he threw one at the eland, and it ran away, and he called it back, and he missed with each of them, and each time called it back, and then he went to his nephew to get arrow-poison, and he was away three days.
>
> While he was away his sons Cogaz and Gewi went out with the young men to hunt, and they came upon the eland their father had hidden, and they did not know about it. It was a new animal. Its horns had just grown, and they tried to encircle it and stab it, and it always broke through the circle and afterwards came back and lay in the same place. At last, while it was asleep, Gewi, who could throw well, pierced it, and they cut it up and took the meat

and blood home; but after they had cut it up they saw the snares and traps of Cagn, and knew it was his, and they were afraid.

And Cagn came back on the third day and saw the blood on the ground where it had been killed, and he was very angry, and he came home and told Gewi he would punish him for his presumption and disobedience, and he pulled off his nose and flung it into the fire.

But he said "No! I shall not do that," so he put the nose on again, and he said, "Now begin to try to undo the mischief which you have done, for you have spoilt the elands when I was making them fit for use," so he told him to take the eland's blood and put it in a pot and churn it . . . and he scattered the blood, and it turned into snakes, and they went abroad, and Cagn told him not to make frightful things, and he churned again and scattered the blood, and it turned into hartebeests, and they ran away, and his father said, "I am not satisfied; this is not yet what I want; you can't do anything. Throw the blood out! Coti, my wife! cleanse this pot and bring more blood from the little paunch where they put it, and churn it," and she did so, and they added the fat from the heart, and she churned it, and he sprinkled it, and the drops became bull elands; and these surrounded them and pushed them with their horns, and he said, "You see how you have spoilt the elands," and he drove those elands away: and then they churned and produced eland cows, and then they churned and produced multitudes of elands, and the earth was covered with them.

And he told Gewi: "Go and hunt them and try to kill one, that is now your work, for it was you who spoilt them," and Gewi ran and did his best, and came back panting and footsore and worn out; and he hunted again next day, and was unable to kill any. They were able to run away because Cagn was in their bones. Then Cagn sent Cogaz to turn the elands back towards him, and Cagn shouted and the elands came running close past him, and he threw assegais [spears] and killed three bulls, and then he sent Cogaz to hunt, and he gave him a blessing, and he killed two, and then he sent Gewi, and he killed one.

That day game were given to men to eat, and this is the way they were spoilt and became wild. Cagn said he must punish them for trying to kill the thing he made which they did not know, and he must make them feel sore.

The ancient Egyptians, according to Aelian, held that the eland, *Taurotragus oryx,* is the first creature to know when the Dog star is rising, and that it signals this by sneezing. For their part, the Greeks believed that only one kind of human could outrun an eland: the Dog Men of Ethiopia, who "are very swift of foot and know the regions that are inaccessible: that is why they are themselves so hard to capture."

Elephant

It is no longer news that animals are being driven to extinction at an astonishing rate, with some scientists now estimating that more than a thousand species disappear each year.

What is news is that the species are increasingly familiar to us: lions, grizzly bears, gorillas, whales, tigers, black terns. Not exactly backyard denizens, to be sure, but more familiar than the anonymous beetles, worms, and slugs that usually slide into extinction when forests are cleared and wetlands paved over, and whose passing usually goes by unremarked save, perhaps, by a few scientists.

Now the elephant, that eminently familiar creature, is at death's door. In the nineteenth century, writes Douglas Chadwick in his study *The Fate of the Elephant,* Africa boasted more than 10 million of the giant pachyderms. There are fewer than half a million today, and their numbers are falling by the day. The situation is similar in Asia, the domain of *Elephas maximus,*

the cousin of the African *Loxodonta africana.* And the cause is nothing more than human vanity.

"Wildlife," Chadwick writes, "is the second most lucrative illegal trade item in the world, exceeded only by drugs." Today hundreds of thousands of elephants are killed each year for the ivory their tusks yield. More than 70 percent winds up in Japan, where the ivory becomes jewelry and especially the personalized signature seals called *hanko,* without which no Japanese business transaction is complete. The rest comes to Europe and America, entombed in desktop ornaments and trinkets that no charity can describe as useful to anyone—yet another example of the banality of evil.

The rush for ivory sees younger and younger elephants slaughtered as the adults are winnowed out. In 1979 it took 54 elephants to secure a ton of ivory. Today it takes 113, and most of those are juveniles on whom the survival of the species depends.

Then there are the comparatively lucky elephants who wind up in zoos. Most are victims of severe arthritis, because to be healthy elephants need to walk twenty or thirty miles a day, and in captivity they cannot. Most are psychologically traumatized as well, for the intelligent and sociable elephant needs constant social contact, with people in the absence of other elephants; in stress, an elephant will swing its trunk back and forth, much as some people grind their teeth. No wonder the elephant at the local zoo looks so miserable.

What is to be done? First, we must initiate and enforce a total ban on the illegal ivory trade—and impose sanctions on strategic, so-called friendly nations like Japan and Singapore, which ignore international conventions to keep the barbarous supply rolling. But much more is needed. Most elephants reside in Third World nations, where a set of tusks can bring a poacher the equivalent of two years' wages. (Consider what would happen to, say, the moose in this country if its antlers were suddenly worth a minimum of $25,000.) If elephants are to survive—and that's a mighty big if—the developed world will have somehow to help developing nations find alternate sources of income. Still more important, we as first-world consumers will have to shed some of our vanity, give up fur coats and ivory pendants and leopardskin rugs. (It almost goes without saying that these items are the province of the rich.) We will have to make room for other species and adjust our ways of life accordingly.

The Bushmen of the Kalahari Desert tell a story that suggests their regard for animals with the utilitarian eye of a hunting people. It seems that Pishiboro, the chief Bushmen deity, was married to an elephant. One day, Pishiboro's brother murdered this elephant wife while delousing her, then built a fire, cut off one of her breasts, and roasted it, eating it from his perch atop her corpse. Pishiboro came upon this scene and was about to slay his brother for his crime, but his brother said, "Hey, stupid! All this time you have been married to meat, and you thought of her as a wife!" Pishiboro pondered this remark and then helped himself to some of the meat, seeing that the brother was correct.

Elephants are tragically vulnerable. Even in ancient times elephants brought as captives from one country to another were presumed to suffer from an unconquerable homesickness, and many of them pined away, some having lost their sight by virtue of the rivers of tears they cried while longing for their homeland.

They are also mild souls, easy marks. As Beryl Markham writes in *West with the Night,* "It is absurd for a man to kill an elephant. It is not brutal, it is not heroic, and certainly it is not easy; it is just one of those preposterous things that men do, like putting a dam across a great river." The gentility of the elephant abounds; Aelian reports that in India, drivers calm an elephant who is off his food with music from an instrument called a *scindapsus*—perhaps the sitar. "Then the elephant is freed from his bonds," Aelian continues, "but remains enchanted by the music, and eats his food with the eagerness of a feasting man, and because of his love for music he will no longer starve himself or run away."

Elephants who have once been tamed revert readily to a wild state, however. Ian Douglas-Hamilton reports that "individuals and groups from areas where they have been shot at relatively little or not at all over the span of the colonial period are comparatively tame, while those from areas where the hunting was intense are shy and dangerous." He also remarks on their prodigious memory, taking as his case in point a curious happening at South Africa's Addo National Park. That memory is cultural, transmitted from generation to generation:

> Here, in 1919, at the request of neighboring citrus farmers, an attempt was made to annihilate a small population of about 140 elephants. A well-known hunter named Pretorius was given the job. Unlike Ian Parker's teams, whose rapid semi-automatic fire liquidated entire family units, Pretorius killed elephants one by one. Each time survivors remained who at the sound of a shot had witnessed one of their family unit members collapsing dead or in its death agonies. . . . Within a space of a year there were only 16 to 30 animals left alive. It seemed that one final push would rid the farmers of their enemies, but by then the remaining elephants had become extremely wary and never came out of the thickest bush until after dark. . . . Pretorius eventually admitted himself beaten and in 1930 the Addo elephants were granted a sanctuary of some 8,000 acres of scrubby hillside. The behavior of these survivors has changed very little, though they have been contained by a fence and are not shot at any more. Even today they remain mainly nocturnal and respond extremely aggressively to any human presence. They are reported to be among the most dangerous elephants in Africa. Few if any of those shot at in 1919 can still be alive, so it

seems that their defensive behavior has been transmitted to their offspring, now adult, and even to calves of the third and fourth generation, not one of which has suffered attack from man.

In his *Historia Naturalis*, which dates to A.D. 77, Pliny is rather less rigorous in his description of pachyderm behavior. The translation is in the marvelous Elizabethan English of Philemon Holland:

Elephants breed in that part of Affricke which lyeth beyond the deserts and wildernesse of the Syrtes: also in Mauretania: they are found also among the Aethiopians and Troglodites, as hath been said: but India bringeth forth the biggest: as also the dragons, that are continually at variance with them, and evermore fighting, and those of such greatnesse, that they can easily claspe and wind around about the Elephants, and withal tye them fast with a knot. In this conflict they die, both the one and the other: the Elephant falls downe dead as conquered, and with his heavie weight crusheth and squeaseth the dragon that is wound and wreathed about him.

Wonderful is the wit and subtiltie that dumb creatures have & how they shift for themselves and annoy their enemies: which is the only difficultie that they have to arise and grow to so great an heigth and excessive bignesse. The dragon therefore espying the Elephant when he goeth to releese, assaileth him from an high tree and launceth himselfe upon him; but the Elephant knowing well enough he is not able to withstand his windings and knittings about him, seeketh to come close to some trees or hard rockes, and so for to crush and squise the dragon between him and them: the dragons ware hereof, entangle and snarle his feet and legges first with their taile: the Elephants on the other side, undoe those knots with their trunke as with a hand: but to prevent that againe, the dragons put in their heads into their snout, and so stop their breath, and withall, fret and gnaw the tenderest parts that they find there. Now in case these two mortall enemies chaunce to reencounter upon the way, they bristle and bridle one against another, and addresse themselves to fight; but the principall thing the dragons make at, is the eye: whereby it cometh to passe, that many times the elephants are found blind, pined for hunger, and worne away, and after much languishing, for very anguish and sorrow die of their venime. What reason should a man alledge of this so mortall warre betweene them, if it be not a verie sport of Nature and pleasure that shee takes, in matching these two so great enemies togither, and so even and equall in every respect? But some report this mutuall war between them after another sort: and that the occasion thereof ariseth from a naturall cause. For (say they) the elephants bloud is exceeding cold, and therefore the dragons be wonderfull desirous thereof to refresh and coole themselves therewith, during the parching and hote season of the yeere. And to this purpose they lie under the water, waiting their time to take the Elephants at a vantage when they are drinking. Where they catch fast hold first of their trunke: and they have not so soone clasped and entangled it with their taile, but they set their venomous teeth in the Elephants eare, (the onely part of all their bodie, which they cannot reach unto with their trunke) and so bite it hard. Now these dragons are so big withall, that they be able to receive all the Elephants bloud. Thus are they sucked drie, untill they fall down dead: and the dragons again, drunken with their bloud, are squised under them, and die both together.

Aristotle writes that the elephant bends its joints inward just as humans do, and does not, as was supposed, sleep standing up; still, Shakespeare could write, in *Troilus and Cressida,* "The elephant hath joints, but none for courtesy; his legs are legs for necessity, not for flexure."

Zaruddin Muhammad Babur, the first Moghul emperor of India, was not only a formidable warrior but also a man driven by curiosity. He writes in his memoir, *The Baburnama,* of the strange flora and fauna of the newly conquered territories, including the elephant:

The elephant is a huge and intelligent animal. It understands what it is told and does what it is ordered to do. . . . It is said that on some islands there are elephants ten yards tall, but recently none larger than four to five yards tall has been seen. . . . Elephants have several good qualities: they can easily carry heavy loads across large and swift-running rivers. Three or four elephants can haul mortar carts that would take four or five hundred men to pull. They eat a lot, however: an elephant eats as much as two strings of camels.

Elephants are famous for their secrecy, which the ancients supposed to be a species of modesty; and they are especially secretive about giving birth, for which reason the ancients also supposed that elephants popped out *sui generis* across the landscape, which has nothing to do with the nineteenth-century American gold miners' expression "seeing the elephant," meaning to view some fantastic and notable sight. Perhaps because of their shyness, regrettably, elephants have more often been studied dead than alive, and zoologists of the past could never quite get a grip on how big their subjects were. As a result, circus posters of the nineteenth century often advertised elephants two stories tall (a figure admittedly still smaller than what Babur reported), when most varieties of elephant do not grow taller than ten feet at the shoulder. As William Hornaday of the American Museum of Natural History remarked, "When a big elephant is dead, probably no man on earth could measure its shoulder height as it lies and hit upon the figure representing its standing height while alive. Nor is it likely that any two men could measure a dead elephant and find their figures for height in agreement. The position of the dead foreleg is a puzzle. As that member lies prone and relaxed in death, it would be almost impossible to know how much to push it up into the shoulder in order to place it just as in life." Hornaday guessed that the average elephant stood about fourteen feet tall.

Of even greater mystery to early naturalists was where elephants go to die. Elephants, they thought, withdraw from society and take themselves off to secret "valleys of ivory" to pass into the beyond; Aelian supposed that the elephants of the Sahara eventually left the desert to ascend the Atlas Mountains and live out their last years alongside pure springs before passing on. (In the Moorish language, by the way, elephant is rendered as *caesai*, "belonging to Caesar," elephants having been introduced to the west African desert by the Romans.) Like most animals, elephants do try to hide when death approaches, perhaps in anticipation of being discovered by predators while in a weakened state, but no one has yet discovered an unknown necropolis for the giants.

Contrary to popular belief, elephants are not especially afraid of mice; as Raymond Ditmars, onetime curator of the New York Zoological Park, wrote, "I have often noted both rats and mice in the hay in circuses and animal shows, and the elephants apparently pay no attention whatever to them." They do show a healthy fear of dogs, and an even healthier fear of humans, as they should. Elephants have been hunted madly for thousands of years, so much so that Edward Topsell, in his *Historye of Four-Footed Beestes* (1607), would take a moment to comment on the still-thriving ivory trade:

> These Ivory teeth have always been of very great estimation among all the Nations that ever knew them, the Ethiopians payed for a tribute unto the King of Persia every third year twenty of these teeth hung about with gold and Jet-wood. These are sold by weight, and there be many which deceive the world with the bones of Fishes in stead thereof, but the true Ivory is paler and heavier, and falling upon the ground will easily break, whereas the bones of Fishes are more tenacious, light and strong. . . . With this ivory they made images and statues for their Idol gods, as one for Pallas in Athens, and for Aesculapias in Epidarus, for Venus under the name of Urania by Phidias, whereupon she was Elephantina, for Apollo at Rome; and therefore Pausanias won-

dereth at the Grecians that spared no cost for the vain worship of their gods, for they brought of the Indians and Ethiopians, Ivory to make their Images with more pomp and ostentation, besides of Ivory they make the hafts of knives, and also the best combs, and Solomon had a throne of Ivory covered all over with gold, for the costs and charge whereof he could not expend lesse than thirty thousand talents.

Elephants are fast disappearing from the wild world, especially in Africa, where they are not generally used as beasts of burden, as they are in southern Asia. The politician Waltari, a character in Romain Gary's novel *The Roots of Heaven*, remarks that Africa has always been the world's zoo and will never have a history until it gets rid of its animals. With the elephant and other animals nearly gone, as I began this essay by remarking, Waltari's dream of a historicized Africa may finally be realized.

Frog

Environmentalists working to protect southern Arizona's San Pedro River from development have long been used to talking in the macrolingo of Big Ideas— biodiversity, sustainability, ecotourism, environmental ethics. They're experts, too, in invoking the Big Picture, as when, in April 1995, the national ecolobbying group American Rivers placed the San Pedro and Gila high on its list of America's most endangered and threatened rivers.

Those environmentalists are taking a smaller view these days. The San Pedro's champions, spearheaded by the Arizona chapter of the Nature Conservancy, have a new poster child in a seemingly unlikely candidate, little in size but not in the scheme of things: the Ramsey Canyon leopard frog (*Rana subaquavocalis*), an eight-inch-long amphibian that turns out to be one of the rarest animals in North America.

Its rarity comes from a curious habit: the Ramsey Canyon leopard frog calls only underwater, and then with an unusually wide repertoire of signals, including a group serenade by which the males attract the females. Biologists have yet to figure out the meaning behind the frog's secretive behavior, but several local researchers are working on the matter.

They may not have much time to figure out why the frogs do what they do. The Ramsey Canyon leopard frog is rare for another reason: there aren't many of them left. Since the discovery of the species just five years ago (*Rana subaquavocalis* was not officially described until 1993), scientists working with the Nature Conservancy have noted a rapid decline in the frog's population: from about a hundred individuals in 1990 to fewer than twenty-five today.

The frog's decline coincides with that of the San Pedro watershed generally. Already heavily taxed by irrigated agriculture and ranching, the San Pedro River faces new threats from urban growth, which is draining the little water that remains. Dr. Robin Silver of the Phoenix-based Southwest Center for Biological Diversity puts the matter baldly. "The river's going dry, there's no doubt," he says. "Without emergent action, it's just a matter of when."

Barely 140 miles long from its headwaters in the Sierra Mariquita of northern Mexico to its confluence with the Gila River southeast of metropolitan Phoenix, the San Pedro hosts the largest remaining area of the rarest type of forest ecosystem in the entire United States, what biologists call the "cottonwood-willow riparian association." More than four hundred bird species, eighty-two mammal species, sixteen fish species, and forty-three reptile and amphibian species, including *Rana subaquavocalis*, make their home along the river.

The rapid growth of the "Fort Huachuca/Sierra Vista complex," in the parlance of regional planners, puts the river and its nonhuman residents in increasing peril. Those planners have foreseen the growth for years; a University of Arizona study from 1981 warned that increased population would effectively kill the river by the year 2020. Sierra Vista's municipal water needs, combined with ranching and agriculture, already use about 22,000 acre-feet (8 billion gallons) of the San Pedro's water a year—nearly the whole of the river's flow.

In 1993, the Department of Defense recommended that Fort Huachuca, now housing a population of about 22,000 soldiers, be expanded to take on 5,000 troops transferred from other posts. That has since been scaled back to some 250 soldiers to be relocated from Fort Ritchey, Maryland, a small figure by most lights, but still more people in an already overpopulated area.

To halt the growth of the fort, the Huachuca Audubon Society has brought a series of legal actions against the federal government. One demands that all federal agencies—among them the departments of Transportation and Housing and Urban Development and the Veteran's Administration—that have any bearing on the fort's future growth not use San Pedro water without consulting with the United States Fish and Wildlife Service and complying with endangered-species regulations.

But that's all Big Picture stuff. Amid this legal and bureaucratic ado, *Rana subaquavocalis* awaits its day of reckoning.

For their part, conservation scientists are trying to improve the odds for the Ramsey Canyon leopard frog. One program now in the works involves reintroducing the once-common beaver to the San Pedro, behind whose dams the frog population once flourished, thanks to the algae-rich ponds those dams formed. Another indirectly related program, one that local biologists don't much like to talk about, involves killing off the huge population of bullfrogs that have been introduced to southern Arizona from Texas and points east over the last century. The bullfrogs have a habit, it seems, of eating whatever local fauna they can, *Rana subaquavocalis* included, and they have become a pest.

The Nature Conservancy has also assembled a "conservation rescue squad" made up of scientists and natural-resource managers from the Arizona Game and Fish Department, Forest Service, Bureau of Land Management, Department of Defense, and other agencies to establish a program of habitat restoration and captive breeding. The immediate aim is to save *Rana subaquavocalis* from extinction, and here the federal government proper may not be of much help: the frog is too recently discovered to fall under federal endangered-species protection, whose waiting list is running years behind schedule.

Should it make that sad roster, the Ramsey Canyon leopard frog may make things a lot harder for those who are hoping to build another Tucson-sized metropolis in Cochise County. Just whose side time is on remains to be seen.

And in any event, all amphibian species around the world are disappearing. Some scientists suggest that the causes of the worldwide decline lie in global warming, chemical contamination, the destruction of the ozone layer and the resulting increase in the intensity of ultraviolet light, and acid rain. More recently, other scientists have posited that an epidemic virus may be afoot and ravaging amphibian populations, although the mechanics of this epidemic have yet to be discovered.

And so we will be left with history, reports on amphibians that we will never see, like the frogs of Mexico that, Gonzalo Fernández de Oviedo y Valdés swore, were "so bigge that the bones of sum of them appear to bee the bones of cattes," and of the Thar Desert of Hindustan, which, says Zaruddin Muhammad Babur, "although are like frogs elsewhere, can run seven or eight yards across the surface of the water."

Gila monster

Every formally trained life scientist in the world is a master of a closed code, a private language: the Linnean binomial system of classification, whereby living things are assigned their place in the universe by the identification of genus and species. (Thus humans, genus *Homo*, species *sapiens*; thus wolves, genus *Canis*, species *lupus*.) The system is named for Carl von Linné (1707–1778), or Linnaeus, an odd man committed to not only the rigor of science and of exact classification but also the slipperiness of numerology, famed for his cranky mystical pronouncements just as much as he was for his undisputed advances in biology.

In his own time, Linnaeus was challenged by other scientists who did not fully accept his insistence on rigid classification. One of his foremost opponents was Georges Louis Buffon (1707–1783), who favored a view of life that concentrated on the individual, then the species, as opposed to Linnaeus's devotion first to the genus, then to the species; it was Buffon who insisted that species be defined in part as a "succession of individuals that can successfully reproduce with each other," a benchmark that is still in general use today. Buffon also insisted on the study of the habits, temperaments, and instincts of animals rather than their gross morphological characteristics, an early holism that carries on in the present practice of natural history.

Neither Linnaeus nor Buffon knew the Americas. Buffon's student and follower Corneille de Pauw, one of whose descendants endowed an American university, did. He did not like the place much. De Pauw wrote in his *Recherches Philosophiques*

sur les Américains (1768) that the lands of the Americas were all deserts, swamps, or mountains, filled with poisonous fogs and death-dealing sun; in that country "monstrous insects grew to prodigious size and multiplied beyond imagining," and the serpents and reptiles were horrendous beyond credulity. Thanks in part to his influence, many of those herps bear terrifying names—like that of the Gila monster, *Heloderma suspectum,* the "suspicious warty-skinned one."

Ignaz Pfefferkorn (1725–1793) spent seven years in Sonora, a province of New Spain that included southern Arizona, as a Jesuit priest among the Eudeve, Opata, and Tohono O'odham peoples. The ruins of the church built for him by the last group may still be seen at Guevavi, near present-day Nogales. Expelled from New Spain with the Jesuit order in 1767, Pfefferkorn returned to his native Germany, where he wrote his book *Beschreibung der Landschaft Sonora* (A Description of the

Province of Sonora). Pfefferkorn found the desert surpassingly strange, and especially the animals that populated it. One of the strangest was the Gila monster, the beaded, venomous lizard that unfortunately has many of the characteristics of the basilisk, that fantastic creature of the medieval Catholic bestiary "which frequents desert places and before people can get to the river it gives them hydrophobia and makes them mad. . . . It can kill with its noise and burn people up, as it were, before it decides to bite them." The legend continued in later years; in *The Faerie Queene,* Edmund Spenser writes of the creature,

> *Like as the basiliske, of serpents seede,*
> *From powerful eyes close venim doth convay*
> *Into the lookers hart, and killeth far away*

and in William Shakespeare's play *Cymbeline,* Posthumus says of the ring given to him as evidence that his wife has been unfaithful,

> *It is a basilisk unto mine eye,*
> *Kills me to look on't.*

Now, Gila monsters are timid, small-jawed creatures, with unfatal eyes. A human has to work to get one to land a bite; still, countless of the reptiles ended up skewered on Spanish lances in an effort to purify the Crown's holdings. (The lancers evidently did not share the belief, which Pliny records, that "once a basilisk was killed with a spear by a man on horseback, the venom passing up through the spear killed not only the rider but the horse as well.") The same fate befell rattlesnakes, "the most villainous kind of beast"; mountain lions, whose "only enemy is the dragon"; tarantulas, wolves, and bears; and innumerable other creatures.

The Gila monster, a "living fossil" far better adapted to the Southwest's temperate past than to its arid present, is still wantonly killed for sport or for its neurotoxic venom, or captured for commercial roadside zoos. An object of hatred since Spanish times, the unfortunate creature had developed a great body of folklore by the time Anglos came to the region. A traveling reporter overheard a drunken cowboy bragging of his exploits with the Gila monster: "I've seed a lizzard what could out-pizen any frog or toad in the world. . . . [My pistol] shot blew the body clean in two, and then I hope to die if the fore-legs didn't get that pistol clean away from me, jump into the [Gila] river and swim away with it." Responding to such stories, one Phoenix doctor remarked, "A man who is foolish enough to get bitten by a Gila monster ought to die."

In Arizona, it is illegal for an individual to own a reticulated Gila monster, but not in California, where the reticulated variety is not resident. Arizona reptile collectors thus take reticulated Gila monsters across the state line, sell them, and then immediately buy them back, so that the creature comes with a California bill of sale. This king-hell mess is becoming a big business, and, as herpetologist Robert McCord observes, "The game laws are almost useless."

The Arizona legislature has not helped much. One lawmaker, a self-described antienvironmentalist named Jeff Groscost, even proposed a bill in 1994 that would allow Gila monster farming. "The rumor right now is that wholesalers are paying up to $900 apiece for them," Groscost argued. "If someone could breed them and raise them in captivity, then you could sell them and not take them out of the wild." He also suggested that the lizards be injected with computer microchips to distinguish them from wild lizards.

Gila monsters being already as rare in the desert as rich people deserving of entry into heaven, any increase in their number should be thought a good thing—but not if the end is simply to fill a collector's cage or a spotter's life list.

Guanaco

It is a longstanding rule of thumb that if you domesticate an animal species, its size will decrease in time: dogs are smaller than wolves, pigs smaller than boars, cats smaller than leopards. The camelids are the great exception to this rule; the camels of the Old World and those of the New (the llama, vicuña, and guanaco) have pretty much held to the size of their wild forebears. Scientists conjecture that the guanaco, a high-desert animal, is the New World ancestor of the llama and the vicuña, whose differences seem to be due to domestication: the llama is chiefly a beast of burden, and the vicuña is chiefly used as a supplier of wool.

Charles Darwin was much taken with the guanaco, as he wrote in his *Voyage of the Beagle*:

> The guanaco, or wild llama, is the characteristic quadruped of the plains of Patagonia; it is the South American representative of the camel of the East. It is an elegant animal in a state of nature, with a long slender neck and fine legs. It is very common over the whole of the temperate parts of the continent, as far south as the islands near Cape Horn. It generally lives in small herds of from half a dozen to thirty in each; but on the banks of the St. Cruz we saw one herd which must have contained at least five hundred.
>
> They are generally wild and extremely wary. Mr. Stokes told me, that he one day saw through a glass a herd of these animals which evidently had been frightened, and were running away at full speed, although their distance was so great that he could not distinguish them with his naked eye. The sportsman frequently receives the first notice of their presence, by hearing from a long distance their peculiar shrill neighing note of alarm. If he then looks attentively, he will probably see the herd standing in a line on the side of some distant hill. On approaching nearer, a few more squeals are given, and off they set at an apparently slow, but really quick canter, along some narrow beaten track to a neighbouring hill. If, however, by chance he abruptly meets a single animal, or several together, they will generally stand motionless

and intently gaze at him; then perhaps move on a few yards, turn round, and look again. What is the cause of this difference in their shyness? Do they mistake a man in the distance for their chief enemy the puma? Or does curiosity overcome their timidity? That they are curious is certain; for if a person lies on the ground, and plays strange antics, such as throwing up his feet in the air, they will almost always approach by degrees to reconnoitre him. It was an artifice that was repeatedly practiced by our sportsmen with success, and it had moreover the advantage of allowing several shots to be fired, which were all taken as parts of the performance. On the mountains of Tierra del Fuego, I have more than once seen a guanaco, on being approached, not only neigh and squeal, but prance and leap about in the most ridiculous manner, apparently in defiance as a challenge. These animals are very easily domesticated, and I have seen some thus kept in northern Patagonia near a house, though not under any restraint. They are in this state very bold, and readily attack a man by striking him from behind with both knees. It is asserted that the motive for these attacks is jealousy on account of their females. The wild guanacos, however, have no idea of defence; even a single dog will secure one of these large animals, till the huntsman can come up. In many of their habits they are like sheep in a flock. Thus when they see men approaching in several directions on horseback, they soon become bewildered, and know not which way to run. This greatly facilitates the Indian method of hunting, for they are thus easily driven to a central point, and are encompassed.

The guanacos readily take to the water: several times at Port Valdes they were seen swimming from island to island. Byron, in his voyage, says he saw them drinking salt water. Some of our officers likewise saw a herd apparently drinking the briny fluid from a salina near Cape Blanco. I imagine in several parts of the country, if they do not drink salt water, they drink none at all. In the middle of the day they frequently roll in the dust, in saucer-shaped hollows. The males fight together; two one day passed quite close to me, squealing and trying to bite each other; and several were shot with their hides deeply scored. Herds sometimes appear to set out on exploring parties: at Bahia Blanca, where, within thirty miles of the coast, these animals are extremely unfrequent, I one day saw the tracks of thirty or forty, which had come in a direct line to a muddy salt-water creek. They then must have perceived that they were approaching the sea, for they had wheeled with the regularity of cavalry, and had returned back in as straight a line as they had advanced. The guanacos have one singular habit, which is to me quite inexplicable; namely, that on successive days they drop their dung in the same defined heap. I saw one of these heaps which was eight feet in diameter, and was composed of a large quantity. This habit, according to M. A. d'Orbigay, is common to all the species of the genus; it is very useful to the Peruvian Indians, who use the dung for fuel, and are thus saved the trouble of collecting it.

The guanacos appear to have favourite spots for lying down to die. On the banks of the St. Cruz, in certain circumscribed spaces, which were generally bushy, and all near the river, the ground was actually white with bones. On one such spot I counted between ten and twenty heads. I particularly examined the bones; they did not appear, as some scattered ones which I had seen, gnawed or broken, as if dragged together by beasts of prey. The animals in most cases must have crawled, before dying, beneath and amongst the bushes. Mr. Bynoe informs me that during a former voyage he observed the same circumstance on the banks of the Rio Gallegos. I do not at all understand the reason of this, but I may observe, that the wounded guanacos at the St. Cruz invariably walked towards the river. At St. Jago in the Cape de Verd islands, I remember having seen in a ravine a retired corner covered with bones of the goat; we at the time exclaimed that it was the burial ground of all the goats in the island. I mention these trifling circumstances, because in certain cases they might explain the occurrence of a number of uninjured bones in a cave, or buried under alluvial accumulations; and likewise the cause why certain animals are more commonly embedded than others in sedimentary deposits.

Darwin was a careful observer of nature, one of the greatest the world has produced, but he seems to have gotten a few things about *Lama guanicoe* wrong. In his memoir *Uttermost Part of the Earth*, a description of life in Tierra del Fuego, E. Lucas Bridges paints a different portrait of the guanaco:

When I was a youngster at Ushuaia, the Governor had a huge dog, half bulldog, half mastiff, which he called Tigre. This monster, whose fierce appearance had been enhanced by the removal of his ears and tail and by the addition of a spiked collar round his great neck, was responsible for the deaths of several dogs that had dared to oppose him, and finally became so dangerous that he had to be shot. Before that timely removal, Tigre had an adventure that must have haunted his dreams until his dying day.

Another possession of his Excellency was a guanaco, very tame and not yet fully grown. It had come from Río Gallegos in Patagonia as a gift from the Governor of that territory. One day this young guest abused his host's hospitality by jumping the fence into the kitchen garden. He was enjoying a feed of fresh, green vegetables when the Governor caught sight of him. This combination of impudence and theft raised his Excellency's ire so much that he summoned the terrible Tigre, opened the garden gate and snapped:

"Chumbale!"

This amounted to an invitation to Tigre to "eat him up," and the dog, nothing loth, plunged forward like a cross between a hippopotamus and a tank, while my brothers and I, who were there at the time, waited breathlessly for the dreadful fate about to overtake the unsuspecting guanaco. At first he did not seem to appreciate his peril. Then, when Tigre was almost upon him, he raised his head with his mouth full of young lettuce—and sailed into the air.

All four feet came down simultaneously on the dog, while the guanaco's teeth sought for a hold on his opponent's tough, round body. Tigre made an effort to stand up to this whirlwind, but after a few fruitless attempts to grab at him, he lost his nerve and rushed back to his master, panic-stricken and yelping for protection, with his enemy pounding after him as he ran.

Ever after that event, though Tigre might be out looking for trouble and ready to challenge any other foe, the sight of that guanaco was enough to send him straight to the shelter of his kennel. As it grew older, the guanaco became as big a nuisance as Tigre, but did not share the same fate. Instead he was sent to the Zoo at Buenos Aires.

I quote this incident to show that the guanaco is not the poor, defenseless creature of popular belief. Even a tame guanaco can be a dangerous beast. In the Botanic Garden at Edinburgh, Scotland, they once had a male guanaco from Patagonia that very seriously injured one of the keepers, who, though a powerful man, would undoubtedly have been killed had his companions not promptly run to his rescue. At the very best, the guanaco is a disagreeable, ill-mannered brute. He chews the cud like a cow, mixing it with saliva, and has the unpleasant habit of spitting out great quantities of the nauseous blend, with unerring aim and in a most insolent manner, right in the face of his visitor.

The long, sharp, canine teeth in the jaws of the grown male might almost be called tusks and, though the student of animal dentistry may say that it is not possible to have more than two canine teeth in one jaw, the guanaco seems to have them in pairs. Perhaps there is a special name for the extra teeth.

While I was on a visit to Buenos Aires, I was invited to lunch by Dr. Holmberg, the director of the fine Zoological Gardens in that city. During our conversation, I happened to mention that there were certain small differences between the guanaco of Patagonia and those on the main island of Tierra del Fuego, and also between the latter and those on Navarin Island. Dr. Holmberg did not attempt to disguise his incredulity. He said that they had a number of Patagonian guanaco in the Zoo and that there had been put with them a Fuegian guanaco so resembling its brethren from Patagonia that not even the keepers could tell them apart. He had been at great pains to assure himself that there was no dissimilarity whatever between the two types.

I took this as a challenge and we went out together to take a look at the troop—about fifteen of them. It did not take me long to decide that there was not a Fuegian guanaco amongst them. I suggested to Dr. Holmberg that the animal he had mentioned had either died or escaped. He smiled at my obstinacy and persisted that the Fuegian guanaco was there before me. He added that it had been sent from Ushuaia as a present to the Zoo.

That explained it. This claimant to Fuegian origin was the same redoubtable warrior as had put the formidable Tigre to flight, the animal who had first seen the light at Rio Gallegos in Patagonia. He must have been at least seventeen years old.

Guanacos, placid or combative creatures as they may be, seem not to have inspired a great body of myth. But, as C. G. Jung says in "On the Relation of Analytical Psychology to Poetry,"

if we are unable to discover any symbolic value in it, we have merely established that, so far as we are concerned, it means no more than what it says, or to put it another way, that it is no more than what it seems to be.

Hedgehog

Hedgehogs abound in Europe, but it took a trip to the Near East as a Crusader to excite the bard Guillaume le Clerc to pen a series of poems about them. Dated to 1208, his *Physiologus* describes other animals—camels, elephants, and dragons—but the hedgehog appears to have been a favorite:

Now we shall tell you of the hedgehog,
Which is like a little pig in shape
When it is a tiny suckling.
Very fully it is armed
For by its nature it has prickles;
And when it hears or sees or feels
Near itself either beast or folk,
Within its armor it shuts and locks itself,
Then fears attack no whit.
From man it cannot defend itself,
But if a beast will seize it
I know not how it could devour it
So badly will it be pricked.

The long-eared hedgehog of Central Asia and other desert hedgehogs seem to be no fiercer, nor less gentle, than their European cousins, but Pliny still says that they "gather food beforehand for the winter; they roll upon fruits lying on the ground, and those that have been caught on their spines they carry away to hollows in trees."

Still, desert hedgehogs are tenacious enough to have merited scientists' naming a human fertility gene after them. The desert

hedgehog gene (Dhh) plays an essential role in sperm production, and the "hedgehog family" of proteins is a newly discovered type of inducing molecules that send genetic messages to cells ordering them to differentiate and mature. Medical reports on Dhh have so far avoided obvious puns on the word *prick*.

Hippopotamus

The ancient Greeks, who took a somewhat fantastic view of nature, averred that the "river horses" they encountered along the desert watercourses of Egypt sweated blood. The hippopotamus does not, of course, but it does have uncommonly thick skin whose pores are full of a thick, reddish oil that has two chief purposes. First, the oil helps the hippopotamus float, a useful trick given that the creature, after the elephant, is the world's largest land mammal. Second, it helps keep the skin itself from drying and cracking under the hot desert sun, an especially helpful trait when water is scarce and the hippopotamus has to head inland. The carmine pigment, as it is called, resembles blood on quick inspection, thus leading ancient zoologists to come to their conclusion.

Horse

The horse is the grasslands creature par excellence. (It is also the creature most mentioned by English speakers in common expressions—horse sense, horse feathers, horse of a different color.) Yet wild horses have been a common denizen, and sometimes a pest, in all the deserts of the world: in the Southwest, where mustangs have run free since the days of the Spanish entrada; in Australia, where desert renegades number in the hundreds of thousands; in Central Asia, where horses were first domesticated. The only significant landmass without horses is, in fact, that desert par excellence, Antarctica, and even there horses have been put to use over the years, hauling sledges over the unforgiving ice.

One desert place where wild horses have not been a problem lately is Turkmenistan. Quite the reverse: for the horsebreeding Turkmeni, even keeping horses was once a problem. The famed Akhal-Teke horse, a fast desert runner descended from an ancestor of the near-extinct Przewalski horse of Mongolia, was outlawed during the regime of Nikita Khrushchev, who decreed that because tractors had been brought to Turkmenistan to complete the Bolshevik agricultural revolution, horses were no longer necessary. He ordered that the horses, descendants of the world's first purebred sires, be destroyed; but Turkmeni herdsmen smuggled a few hundred into the hills and quietly continued breeding them, biding their time until the inevitable collapse of Communism. That collapse came, and the Akhal-Teke, now being bred openly, is the symbol of the newly independent Republic of Turkmenistan.

In Navajo belief, the sun is carried across the sky by wild horses of different colors. When he rides his turquoise horse, the sky is blue; when the sun rides his white horse, the sky is full of soft clouds; and when he rides his black horse, the sky is charged with rain and thunder.

Hummingbird

One of the finest desert oases I know once lay along the banks of the Gila River just outside the small town of Winkelman, Arizona. An elderly Mexican American woman lived in a small frame house perhaps twenty yards from the stream, separated by a grove of cottonwoods in whose branches she had hung dozens of hummingbird feeders. Those feeders drew hundreds of hummingbirds from all around, so many that approaching her house within a hundred yards you would swear you were entering a beehive. I spent many hours on the riverbank near her house, watching the birds and making notes for a book I was writing on the natural and human history of the Gila.

All but dead thanks to damming and overuse, that river came to life with a vengeance in 1993, roaring through Winkelman and destroying all in its path. The woman's house, the cotton-woods, and the hummingbird feeders disappeared in a wall of water. Where the woman went I do not know, but I hope she has made another oasis in the desert to give weary travelers a little pleasure.

When Georges Louis Leclerc, the Comte de Buffon (*see* Gila monster), first heard tales of the hummingbird, a lover of heat and sun, he was hard put to find a place for it in his order of things. He did compose, however, a fine and lyrical description of the creature he called the Fly-bird in his *Natural History* (1749–1767):

It is in the hottest part of the new world that all the species of Fly-birds are found. They are numerous, and seem confined between the two tropics; for those which penetrate in summer within the temperate zones make but a short stay. They follow the course of the sun; with him they advance or retire; they fly on the wings of the zephyr, to wanton in eternal spring.

The Indians, struck with the dazzle and glow of the colors of these brilliant birds, have named them the beams or locks of the sun. The Spaniards call them *tomineos,* on account of their diminutive size, *tomine* signifying a weight of twelve grains. "I saw," says Nieremberg, "one of these birds weighed with its nest, and the whole together did not amount to two tomines." The smaller species do not exceed the bulk of the great gad-fly, or the thickness of the drone. Their bill is a fine needle, and their tongue a delicate thread; their little black eyes resemble two brilliant points; the feathers of their wings are so thin as to look transparent; hardly can the feet be perceived, so short they are and so slender: and these are little used, for they rest only during the night. Their flight is buzzing, continued, and rapid; Marcgrave compares the noise of their wings to the whirr of a spinning-wheel; so rapid is the quiver of their pinions, that when the bird halts in the air, it seems at once deprived of motion and of life. Thus it rests a few seconds beside a flower, and again shoots to another like a gleam. It visits them all, thrusting its little tongue into their bosom, and caressing them with its wings; it never settles, but it never quite abandons them. Its playful inconstancy multiplies its innocent pleasures; for the dalliance of this little lover of flowers never spoils their beauty. It only sips their honey, and its tongue seems

calculated for that purpose; it consists of two hollow fibres, form-
ing a small canal, parted at the end into two filaments: it resembles
the proboscis of insects, and performs the same office. The bird
protrudes it from its bill, probably by a mechanism of the *os
hyoides,* similar to what obtains in the tongue of woodpeckers. It
thrusts it to the bottom of the flowers, and sucks their juices. Such
is its mode of subsisting according to all the authors who have
written on the subject. One person alone denies the fact; he is
Badier, who, finding in the oesophagus some portions of insects,
concludes that the bird lives on these, and not the nectar of flowers. But we cannot reject a number of respectable authorities for
a single hasty assertion; though the Fly-bird swallows some
insects, does it thence follow that it subsists upon them? Nay, must
it not necessarily happen, that, sucking the honey from the flowers, or gathering their pollen, it will sometimes swallow the little
insects which are entangled? Besides, the rapid waste of its spirits,
the consequence of its extreme vivacity and its rapid incessant
motion, must continually be recruited by rich nutritious aliments:
and Sloane, on whose observations I lay the greatest stress, posi-
tively avers that he found the stomach of the Fly-bird entirely
filled with the pollen, and Sweet juice of flowers.

Nothing can equal the vivacity of these little creatures, but their
courage, or rather audacity: they furiously pursue birds twenty
times larger than themselves, fix in the plumage, and as they are
hurried along strike keenly with the bill, till they vent their feeble rage: Sometimes even they fight obstinately with each other.
They are all impatience; if upon alighting in a flower they find it
faded, they will pluck the petals with a precipitation that marks
their displeasure. Their voice is only a feeble cry, *screp, screp,*
which is frequent and reiterated. They are heard in the woods at
the dawn of the morning, and as soon as the sun begins to gild
the summits of the trees, they take wing and disperse in the fields.

They are solitary; and indeed, fluttering irregularly in the
breeze, they could hardly associate. But the power of love sur-
mounts the elements, and, with its golden chains, it binds all

animated beings. The Fly-birds are seen to pair in the breeding season: their nest corresponds to the delicacy of their bodies; it is formed with the soft cotton or silky down gathered from flowers, and has the consistency and feel of a thick smooth skin. The female performs the work, and the male collects the materials. She applies herself with ardor; selects, one by one, the fibers proper to form the texture of this kindly cradle for her progeny; she smoothes the margin with her breast, the inside with her tail; she covers the outside with bits of the bark of the gum-tree, which are stuck to shelter from the weather, and give solidity to the fabric: the whole is attached to two leaves, or a single sprig of the orange or citron, or sometimes to a straw hanging from the roof of a hut. The nest is not larger than the half of an apricot, and it is also shaped like a half cup. It contains two eggs, which are entirely white, and not exceeding the bulk of small peas. The cock and hen sit by turn twelve days; on the thirteenth the young are excluded, which are then not larger than flies. "I could not perceive," says Father Dutertre, "how the mother fed them, except that she presented the tongue covered entirely with honey extracted from the flowers."

We may easily conceive that it is impossible to raise these little flutterers. Those who have tried to feed them with syrups could not keep them alive more than a few weeks: these aliments, though of easy digestion, are very different from the delicate nectar collected from the fresh blossoms. Perhaps honey would have succeeded better.

Hyena

If there were ever an animal more maligned than the hyena, I do not know what it is. The bad press dates at least to the time of Pliny, who writes in the *Natural History* that by listening to men talking together the hyena will learn the name of one of them, and then call to that man in a humanlike voice, luring him to his death. Hyenas lack any such powers, we now know. Indeed, only humans kill with a complete knowledge of the pain they may inflict.

Jane Goodall, the famed student of chimpanzee society, and Hugo van Lawick studied hyenas in the 1960s in the arid Serengeti Plain of Tanzania. In their book *Innocent Killers* they note that the hyena is an efficient, sometimes bold predator, far from being the slinking scavenger that he has been made out to be; its ecological cousin, the genetically unrelated jackal, a more generalized scavenger, spends even more time hunting after insects and rodents than in finding castoff food to steal. In the Serengeti ecosystem, they note, the hyena plays the role of the wolf, while the jackal is more like the bear, cumbersome, slow, yet fierce. And, like the wolf, the hyena lives in social clans that comprise as many as a hundred individuals who carefully mark their territories and guard them against incursions by members of other clans.

The hyenas of the eastern Sahara desert are hunters and scavengers like other hyenas, but evidently more pliant in the face of religious instruction, as this anecdote from the *Lives of the Desert Fathers* shows, relating the miracle effected by one monk:

It happened one day as he was sitting in his cell, a hyaena came to him, her whelp was in her mouth; she set it down beside the door, she knocked on the door with her head. The old man heard her knock, and he came out thinking that a brother had come to him. When he opened the door he saw the hyaena, he was astounded, saying, "What does she want here?" She filled her mouth with her whelp, she held it out to the old man, weeping. The old man took the whelp in his hands, steady in simplicity, he turned it this way and that, looking in its body for what ailed it. When he had considered the whelp, behold, it was blind in its two eyes. He took it, he groaned, he spat on its face, he signed it on

the eyes with his finger: straightway the whelp saw, it went to its
mother's dug, it sucked, it followed her, they went away to that
river . . . and into the marsh they made their way. The sheep of
the Lybians, they bring them once each year into the marsh of
Scete to eat the *shoushet,* and the herdsmen that live in the villages
over against Pernouj, they also bring their oxen into the marsh of
Scete to eat the green herbage, once a year.

The hyaena left a day behind her. The next day she came to the
old man, she had a sheepskin in her mouth, thick with wool, freshly
killed, she had it over her; she struck the door with her head.

The old man was sitting in the enclosure. When he heard the
knock at the door, he got up, he opened it: he found the hyaena,
the sheepskin over her. He said to the hyaena, "Where hast thou
been? Where hast thou found this, if thou hast not eaten a sheep?
As that which thou hast brought me comes of violence, I will not
take it."

The hyaena struck her head upon the ground, she bent her
paws, and on her knees she prayed him, as if she had been a man,
to take it. He said to her, "I have but now told thee that I will not
take it unless thou makest me this promise: I will not vex the poor
by eating their sheep." She made many movements of her head,
up and down, as if she were promising him. Again he repeated it
to her, saying, "Unless thou dost promise me, saying, I will not
kill a creature alive; from to-day thou wilt eat thy prey when it is
dead. If thou art distressed, seeking and finding none, come
hither, and I will give thee bread. From this hour, do hurt to no
creature." And the hyaena bowed her head to the ground, and
dropped on her knees, bending her paws, moving her head up and
down, looking at his face as if she were promising him. And the
old man perceived in his heart that it was the purpose of God
Who gives understanding to beasts for a reproach unto ourselves,
and he gave glory to God Who gives understanding to the beasts,
he sang in the Egyptian tongue God, Who liveth for ever, for the
soul hath honour: he said, "I give glory to Thee O God Who
wast with Daniel in the lion's den, Who didst give understanding
unto beasts: also Thou hast given understanding to this hyaena
and Thou hast not forgotten me: but Thou hast made me perceive

that it is Thy ordering." And the old man took the skin from the hyaena, and she went away. From time to time she would come to seek the old man; if she had not been able to find food, she would come to him and he would throw her a loaf. She did this many a time. And the old man slept on the skin until he died. And I have seen it with my own eyes.

Many writers have commented on the hyenas' loathsome smell, and on their fondness, shared with dogs and other carnivores, for rolling around in stench-drenched objects like carrion and offal. Still, notes Jane Goodall, "considering that the foundation for so many expensive perfumes comes from the anal glands of civets, perhaps we should not be too surprised at or critical of the hyena's taste in suitable odors."

Aristotle, who almost certainly never saw one up close, correctly observes that the hyena and jackal are both nearly hairless in the summer, but in the winter sport thick coats of fur. Less accurately, he remarks in his *History of Animals* that the hyena "has in its left paw the power of sending to sleep and can with a mere touch induce stupor. It often visits stables, where it lays its paw on animals' noses, and suffocates them. In the meanwhile it scoops out the earth underneath the animal, and lays it down with its head dangling in the hole, and grabs the animal by its neck and drags it off to its lair. It also attacks dogs like this: when the moon is full, the hyena gets its rays behind him so that the moon's shadow, mixed with his, is cast on the dogs. This bewitches them, and the hyena then carries them off tongue-tied to do with them whatever he will."

Elsewhere, Aristotle remarks that the hyena attracts dogs for its dinner by imitating the sound of a man vomiting. His follower Pliny adds that the gall of a hyena will cure bleary eyes, and that if a hyena turns around on the tracks of whatever man or beast is hunting it, the pursuer will grow dizzy and fall down.

Jackrabbit

Coyote is, in Western North America, the primary trickster figure. There Rabbit, a principal of trickster tales throughout the world, and especially Africa, does not often have the chance to come out on top of the various schemes the world hatches; but here, in this Tohono O'odham story collected by the linguist Daniel Matson, he outsmarts Coyote with painful result:

It happened hereabouts once upon a time
that a rabbit was sitting somewhere
and then a coyote came,
so the rabbit started to push against the rock.
The coyote said:
"I am going to eat you, Rabbit."
And the rabbit said:
"Pity me and do not eat me,
because this rock will fall upon us and kill us."
Then the rabbit continued:
"If you will push against this rock
I will run and fetch a cheese
from over there behind the mountain."
The coyote believed the rabbit
and pushed against the rock,
and the rabbit ran away.
The coyote just watched the rabbit going.
Then the coyote said to himself
that he might just let go of the rock
and run off.
So he let go of the rock and ran fast

and the rock did not fall over.
The coyote became very angry.
He said:
"If I find the rabbit somewhere again
I will eat him."
So time went on
and somewhere he again came
to where the rabbit was sitting.
He just said:
"This time I will eat you
because you lied to me."
Then the rabbit also spoke:
"Pity me and do not eat me
and I will lead you to where
you can eat meat;
and if anyone there wants to dance
you can dance."
And the coyote liked this.
And the rabbit said:
"I am also going to melt some mesquite gum.
You shall swallow this much of it;
and when you hear the fireworks you must dance hard
and also yell loud."
And the coyote also liked this.
So they walked until they came to a place
that was full of reeds.
And the rabbit stuck the eyes of the coyote with resin.
Then he set fire to the reeds.
And there were very many reeds
and they crackled loud.
And the coyote danced hard
and yelled loud.
When it got hot
the coyote just said to himself:
that it was hot

because he was dancing hard;
but he was really burning.

In another O'odham legend, the jackrabbit and deer were among the first of earth's creatures, brought into existence so that the People might have something to eat. The Creator sang this song after making this larder:

The gray jackrabbit, the gray jackrabbit,
This is for you, this is for you.
The earth looks like a mirage,
Water all over.

Mark Twain, in *Roughing It*, adds to the body of jackrabbit lore with this altogether anthropomorphic description:

As the sun was going down, we saw the first specimen of an animal known familiarly over two thousand miles of mountain and desert—from Kansas clear to the Pacific Ocean—as the "jackass rabbit." He is well named. He is just like any other rabbit, except that he is from one-third to twice as large, has longer legs in proportion to his size, and has the most preposterous ears that ever were mounted on any creature but a jackass. When he is sitting quiet, thinking about his sins, or is absent-minded or unapprehensive of danger, his majestic ears project above him conspicuously; but the breaking of a twig will scare him nearly to death, and then he tilts his ears back gently and starts for home. All you can see, then, for the next minute, is his long gray form stretched out straight and "streaking it" through the low sage-brush, head erect, eyes right, and ears just canted a little to the rear, but showing you where the animal is, all the time, the same as if he carried a jib. Now and then he makes a marvelous spring with his long legs, high over the stunted sagebrush, and scores a leap that would make a horse envious. Presently he comes down to a long, graceful "lope," and shortly he mysteriously disappears. He has crouched behind a sage-bush, and will sit there and listen and tremble until you get within six feet of him, when he will get under way again. But one must shoot at this creature once, if he wishes to see him throw his heart into his heels, and do the best he knows how. He is frightened clear through, now, and he lays his long ears down on his back, straightens himself out like a yard-stick every spring he makes, and scatters miles behind him with an easy indifference that is enchanting.

Australians have been less than enchanted with the rabbits that their forebears introduced and that, lacking predators, bred far beyond anyone's expectations. A dozen members of the principal breed were brought to Victoria in 1859 and let loose to reproduce, and so they did: by 1950, Australia had a population of more than 600 million rabbits. Evidently not having seen

Terry Gilliam's cautionary film *Twelve Monkeys,* Australian scientists released an experimental virus in late 1995 that has wiped out rabbits by the hundreds of thousands. In Flinders Ranges National Park, rangers counted 850,000 dead rabbits in a single day. One ranger commented, "Most rabbit deaths, according to the scientists, are supposed to occur under the ground. So the figure for dead rabbits taken off the park is horrendous."

This is not the first time the Australian government has conducted biological warfare against rabbits. In 1954—coincidentally, at the height of British government testing of nuclear weapons in the Australian desert—scientists released myxomatosis, a virus first isolated in South America, which killed nearly 500 million rabbits in just a few years. Over time, however, the survivors built up immunity and nearly restored their numbers. The new rabbit killer, calicivirus, is spreading in an unexpected way; scientists on an island off the southern coast infected a captive population of rabbits, and some of the insects who bit them were carried by unusually strong winds onto the mainland. In just a few weeks, the virus spread across the continent. Attempts to isolate it have failed.

How the cruel virus, which causes rabbits to hemorrhage internally, will mutate is anyone's guess. Take in Gilliam's film, perhaps along with a showing of the spectacularly bad *Night of the Lepus,* and fear for the worst.

Kangaroo

It took a long time for scientists to categorize kangaroos, so strange did they appear to taxonomists trained in the Linnean system. Lay people had little clearer understanding of *Macropus rufus*, it would appear; as Paul Shepard remarks in his book *The Others*, "Manatees, dugongs, armadillos, or pangolins, encountered by the individual after the closure of the taxonomic mindset (at about age eleven), have no affiliation. So it was that the European travelers in Australia named the animals and the birds as if they were bizarre combinations, such as the duck-billed platypus, the wren-tits, and the whole panoply of marsupial 'cats,' 'wolves,' 'rats,' and so on." Neither cat, wolf, nor rat, but sharing qualities with all of these animals, the assuredly marsupial kangaroo remained an object of mystery.

Animals like the marsupial lion and Tasmanian wolf did not survive the arrival of humans in Australia; aboriginal hunters eventually exterminated both species, the continent's most prominent megafaunal predators, and hence became the chief objects of fear in the Australian menagerie. Kangaroos were more successful in this war of survival of the fittest. According to the late animal physiologist C. Richard Taylor, this was the case because kangaroos burned less energy when hopping than when walking or running, as lions and wolves moved, and could therefore flee from approaching predators more efficiently. Taylor proved this by a decades-long research campaign that involved laboratories full of kangaroos on treadmills; while he was working out this problem, he incidentally showed that the eland and the oryx could survive the heat of the Australian desert by regulating their metabolism and feeding on water-rich shrubs.

Aboriginal legend, not surprisingly, is shot through with stories of kangaroos. The evil Walawag Sisters, robbers of honey and dessicators of water sources, feed almost exclusively on raw, wormy kangaroo meat. In many dreamings, Kangaroo leads people to water and shows them where to make their homes. One Western Desert story about Malu, Kangaroo, holds him and his ritual descendants responsible for naming places on the land in a kind of second dreaming, or second creation, an event honored by the *ubar* ritual. One of the informants to anthropologists Ronald and Catherine Berndt described this ritual so:

All the Kangaroo Men lined up and began to jump around and around in a haunched posture, propelling themselves with their arms as kangaroos do, and they saw that their dancing was all right. Then they brought out one man and sat him by himself in the middle of the ground. He began to shiver ritually like an owl. After watching this performance they said, "Ah, that's very good." They got two more "owls." When they had seen them dancing they said, "In future, you two must always come and dance." Many men were there, but these two were especially good. "We shall call this ritual the *ngurlmag ubar*, it is the most sacred," they said. "*Ngurlmag! Ngurlmag!* Oh Sacred Uterus of our Mother!" The Goanna got ready for his dance.... Then they brought out Blanket Lizard and covered him completely with bushes. The other men got together, chanting loudly, "Ah! Ah! ..." and Blanket Lizard stirred in his hiding place. Singing, and the drone of the didjeridu, continued as the Old Kangaroo took up a different pair of beating sticks and walked over to where Blanket Lizard was hidden. The singing and the didjeridu stopped, and the Old Kangaroo began to beat the sticks as he bent over the other and called the sacred names referring to him.... Lizard emerged, throwing aside his bushes, and danced all the

way down the sacred ground to the sound of the clapping sticks.
. . . Then, while the *ubar* gong was beaten, the Old Kangaroo
called the power names of the sacred totems:

"I name the blue sky, *bajangudjangul*."

"I name the sacred *ubar*, *ubar banagaga*."

"I name the very old woman, *ngalwariwari*."

"I name the moon, *wombidjid*."

"I name the scorpion, *bidjarabul*."

"I name the long bark fire-torch, *djadagulan*."

"I name the barramundi fish, *balgungbi*." And so on.

When he had finished, the men said, "Everything is all right
now!" The *ubar* stopped. The spirit of the Mother had returned
to her own camp. The men went back to the main camp, calling
out to let the women know they were coming. This is why we
perform the *ubar* now.

For what it's worth to experimentally-minded chefs, the traditional aboriginal method of cooking kangaroo is to singe it all
over, distributing the bloody rare meat to the assembled diners,
or else to roast it in underground sand ovens, the kangaroo
completely covered except for the protruding legs, underdone
drumsticks that are the prime cut of the meal. The Gunwinggu
hold as a special delicacy a dish made up of mashed wild plums
and the marrow and minced meat of a kangaroo. And concoc-
tions like kangaroo rump steak with Tasmanian pepperberry
sauce are now showing up on the menus of posh Australian
restaurants. Proponents note that the meat is low in fat and cho-
lesterol, but that does not stop a prominent conservationist,
Marjorie Wilson, from countering, "We believe that we have
enough meat in this country to satisfy people without them having to eat their national symbol. You Americans don't cook
your bald eagle, do you?"

Had they encountered kangaroos before the first dreaming,
however, the aboriginal peoples might have picked a different

culinary treat. The fossil evidence shows that ancestral kanga- roos—which were arboreal, strangely enough—had long, sharp fangs and claws. They also stood as tall as grizzly bears, and seem to have been just as well equipped for a fight.

Kangaroo skin was once widely collected for the fine-grained leather it yielded. Before World War II nearly a million skins found their way to the United States for the manufacture of shoes, gloves, wallets, and purses, a popularity that led to a booming market in fake kangaroo leather, a happy enough event, one supposes, for the remaining real kangaroos.

Alfred Hitchcock once said, "If I were to make another pic- ture set in Australia, I'd have a policeman hop into the pocket of a kangaroo and yell, 'Follow that car!'"

Kangaroo rat

> *Everything in the mind is in rat's country. It doesn't die. They are merely carried, these disparate memories, back and forth in the desert of a billion neurons, set down, picked up, and dropped again by mental pack rats.*
>
> **Loren Eiseley**

Kangaroo rat is the favorite food of the ringtail (*Bassariscus astu- tus*), a member of the raccoon family that haunts the ghost towns of the Sonoran Desert. It is also a favorite snack for snakes, which led Edward Ricketts, the naturalist hero of John Steinbeck's *Log from the Sea of Cortez*, to muse on the evolu- tionary path that brought these two creatures together. Ricketts concluded, "You know, at first glance you would think the

rattlesnake and the kangaroo rat were the greatest of enemies since the snake hunts and feeds on the rat. But in a larger sense they must be the best of friends. The rat feeds the snake and the snake selects out the slow and weak and generally thins the rat people so that both species can survive. It is quite possible that neither species could exist without the other."

The Navajo tell this story about *Dipodomys*: One day Kangaroo Rat met Bear, who chased him. Kangaroo Rat set fire to Bear's fur in retaliation, and Bear could not put it out. Bear then gave four magical songs to Kangaroo Rat, begging him to put out the fire. So now if you carry Kangaroo Rat fur with you when you travel, no Bear will attack you.

That is useful knowledge indeed for travelers in bear country.

Marianne Moore writes of the kangaroo rat's cousin, the jerboa of North Africa, which

honors the sand by assuming its color;
> *closed upper paws seeming one with the fur*
> *in its flight from a danger.*
By fifths and sevenths,
in leaps of two lengths,
> *like the uneven notes*
> *of the Bedouin flute, it stops its gleaning*
> *on little wheel castors, and makes fern-seed*
> *foot-prints with kangaroo speed.*

The jerboa was known to the ancient Greeks, too, perhaps through Egyptian zoos. Theophrastus remarks, "There are mice in the desert with only two legs, and they grow to a great size. Their front legs they use as hands, for they are much shorter than their back legs. And they walk erect on their two back legs, and when pursued they jump."

Leopard

Come with me from the summit of Amana,
from the top of Senir and Hermon,
from the lions' lairs,
and the leopard-haunted hills.

Song of Songs

Like the other big cats, leopards are fast disappearing from their traditional habitats throughout Africa and Asia, having long since been eradicated from Europe. Only in Mongolia does one variety, the snow leopard, seem to be holding ground, and that is in large measure thanks to a $2 billion project financed by the United Nations–sponsored Global Environmental Facility to set aside great tracts of the Gobi Desert for a biodiversity protection zone. The pressures within the new free-market economy of Mongolia to develop this very area have been great, and only time will tell whether our descendants will be able to see the leopard and its kindred outside of the confines of a zoo.

Aelian writes that "the hunting of leopards is a Moorish practice. The people build a stone structure that resembles a cage, inside which they put a piece of rotting meat. This animal loves the smell of putrid objects, which comes to them in the desert or on a mountaintop or in a canyon or even in the forest, and then the leopard becomes excited and rushes to the spot where the rotting meat lies, as if drawn by a spell. It rushes, as I say, in and begins to gobble the meat, around which a noose has been ingeniously fastened. As the leopard eats the noose winds itself around him and strangles him. So it is caught and pays the price for his gluttony, the miserable wretch."

Lion

"A lion, though he is king of the beasts, is harassed by the tiny tail of the scorpion, and the poison of desert snakes kills him immediately." Thus a Byzantine bestiary, reporting on the lions of Ethiopia, "the place of burned faces." The text goes on to tell us that lions fear only one thing in the world, and that is an albino rooster.

David Livingstone (1813–1873), who arrived in the South African desert in 1841, had ample opportunity to study the behavior of lions up close. One came very close, in fact, and Livingston seems not to have had an albino rooster at hand:

> Starting, and looking half round, I saw the lion just in the act of springing upon me. I was upon a little height; he caught my shoulder as he sprang, and we both came to the ground below together. Growling horribly close to my ear, he shook me as a terrier dog does a rat. The shock produces a stupor similar to that which seems to be felt by a mouse after the first shake of the cat. It caused a sort of dreaminess, in which there was no sense of pain nor feeling of terror, though quite conscious of all that was happening. It was like what patients partially under the influence of chloroform describe, who see all the operation, but feel not the knife. This singular condition was not the result of any mental process. The shake annihilated fear, and allowed no sense of horror in looking round at the beast. This peculiar state is probably produced in all animals killed by the carnivora; and if so, is a merciful provision by our benevolent Creator for lessening the pain of death.

Meriwether Lewis, traveling in Montana, came less uncomfortably close to *Felis concolor,* the mountain lion:

In returning, my direction led me directly to an animal that I at first supposed was a wolf; but on nearer approach or about sixty paces distant I discovered that it was not. Its color was a brownish yellow; it couched itself down like a cat looking immediately at me as if it designed to spring on me. I took aim at it and fired. It instantly disappeared in its burrow. I loaded my gun and examined the place, which was dusty, and saw the track from which I am still further convinced that it was of the tiger kind. It now seemed to me that all the beasts of the neighborhood had made a league to destroy me, or that some fortune was disposed to amuse herself at my expense, for I had not proceded more than three hundred yards from the burrow of this tiger cat, before three bull buffalo, which were feeding with a large herd about half a mile from me, separated from the herd and ran full speed towards me. I altered my direction to meet them; when they arrived within a hundred yards they made a halt, took a good view of me and retreated with precipitation. I then continued my route homewards past the buffalo which I had killed, but did not think it prudent to remain all night at this place which really from the succession of curious adventures wore the impression on my mind of enchantment; at sometimes for a moment I thought it might be a dream, but the prickly pears which pierced my feet convinced me that I was really awake.

A medieval Latin bestiary had more distanced regard for *Panthera leo*: "It is written that the lion is of such a nature that when he is hunted he wipes out with his tail the traces of his footsteps as he goes along, so that none can follow him. The track of the lion typifies the Incarnation. For thus did God lower himself by degrees through the orders of prophets and apostles until he became fleshly man and thus vanquished the Devil. If the Devil had known that God was to become mortal man, he would never have led him on so far as to crucify Him. So God acted cunningly and without being perceived."

Imperceptible or not, folk tradition since antiquity has held the lion to have a hot nature, for which reason, as Aelian observes, "the Lion is the house of the Sun, and when the sun is at its hottest and at the height of summer, they say it is approaching the Lion."

The lion has also been favored game for millennia. Says one ancient Akkadian tablet, "I am Ashurbanipal, king of hosts, king of Assyria [ca. 883–852 B.C.]. In my abounding, princely strength I seized a lion of the desert by his tail, and at the command of Enurta and Nergal, the gods who are my helpers, I smashed his skull with the ax in my hands." The tables, however, have occasionally been turned. Ancient historians recall a tale of a Libyan tribe called the Nomaei who "were wiped out when a vast horde of Lions of the largest size and of irresistible boldness attacked them. The whole race to a man was destroyed by the Lions and perished utterly." The chronicler went on to add, helpfully, "A visitation by Lions in a mass is something that no creature can withstand."

Aelian tells two stories about the lion, the first involving a singular visitation:

> The Lion knows how to take vengeance on one who has previously done him an injury, and even though the vengeance be not immediate, yet doth he keep his anger thereafter in his bosom, until he accomplish it.
>
> Juba of Mauretania . . . bears witness to this. He was marching once through the desert against some tribes who had revolted, when one of the youths who ran beside him, well-born, handsome, and already fond of the chase, struck with a javelin a Lion that chanced to appear by the roadside: he hit the mark and wounded the beast, but failed to kill it. But the expedition was in haste; the animal drew off, and the boy who had wounded it

hurried by with the rest. Now when a whole year had passed and Juba had accomplished his purpose, returning by the same way he arrived at the spot where the Lion had happened to be wounded. And in spite of the multitude of men that same Lion came forward and, without touching anyone else, seized him who a year ago had wounded it, and pouring forth the gathered anger which it had been nursing all that while, tore to pieces the boy whom it had recognized. But not a soul took vengeance: they were afraid of the fierce and absolutely terrifying anger of the Lion. And besides, their journey made them hasten.

The second story reports the little-known Libyan origins of the famous story of Androcles and the Lion, which has long passed into the canon of European literature:

That memory is an attribute even of animals, and that this is a characteristic acquired without the system and science of mnemonics which certain wonder-workers claim to have invented, the following facts demonstrate. One Androcles by name who happened to be a slave in the household of a Roman senator, ran away from his master after committing some offence, the nature and extent of which I am unable to state. Well, he arrived in Libya and was for avoiding towns and, as the saying is, "marked their places only by the stars" and went on into the desert. And being parched by the excessive and fiery heat of the sun, he was glad to take refuge and to rest under a caverned rock. This rock, it seems, was the lair of a Lion.

The Lion returned from hunting, injured from having been pierced with a sharp stake, and when it encountered the young man it looked at him in a gentle manner and began to fawn on him, extending its paw and imploring him as best it could to have the stake plucked out. Androcles at first shrank back. But when he saw that the beast was in gentle mood, and realized what was the matter with its paw, he extracted what was hurting it and rid the Lion of its pain. The Lion therefore in joy at being healed paid him his fee by treating him as its guest and friend, and shared with him the spoils of its chase. And while the Lion ate its food raw, as is the custom of lions, Androcles used to cook his for himself. And they enjoyed a common table each as was his nature. And this was how Androcles lived for the space of three years. After a time, as his hair grew to an excessive length and he was troubled with a violent itching, he forsook the Lion and trusted himself to fortune. Then as he was wandering about he was caught, questioned as to whom he belonged to, and sent bound to his master in Rome. The master punished Androcles for the injury he had done, and he was condemned to be given to the wild beasts to eat. It happened that the same Libyan lion had also been caught and was let loose in the arena together with the young man destined for death, who had shared that very Lion's home and dwelling. The man for his part did not know the Lion again, but the animal immediately recognized the man, fawned on him, and letting his whole body sink down, threw itself at his feet. At last Androcles recognized his friend and threw his arms around the Lion, greeting it as a comrade returned after a long absence. But as he was thought to be a magician, a leopard was then set on him. When the leopard rushed at Androcles, the Lion came to the rescue and tore the leopard to pieces. The spectators, as you might expect, were dumbstruck, and the master of the games called Androcles over and asked him what had happened. The story spread throughout the audience, and on learning the truth they demanded that both Androcles and the Lion be set free.

The ancient Egyptians believed that the best way for a human to be reincarnated was as a lion.

Millipede

Only six percent of the living beings on Earth are vertebrates, but they are the ones we, perhaps because we are also vertebrates, are most concerned with. The creatures from other orders, like the often overlooked desert millipedes, need to assert themselves mightily in order to draw attention to their mere existence. They did so two thousand years ago, when millipedes overran Rhoeteum, a town on the Troad in the high desert of southwestern Turkey, and drove its human inhabitants into the sea.

In the Sonoran Desert the millipede *Orthoporus ornatus* has only one enemy, the venomous larva of the *Zarrhipis* beetle. This larva is luminescent, and it makes for a strange sight indeed to see it wriggle after its slow-moving target in blackest night.

Strange to say, too, but millipedes are vulnerable to heat-stroke.

Ostrich

Goats may be famed in contemporary folklore for their diet of tin cans and tire rims, but in ancient times, the ostrich was renowned for its putatively amazing digestive abilities. Aelian thought that the ostrich lived on the very rocks of the stony desert, the *deserta saxa,* of Arabia, and an ancient bestiary appends the humoral notion that "he swallows even glowing iron and fiery coals, all of which do good for his belly, for by his nature the ostrich is a very cold animal."

In his *Pseudodoxia Epidemica* (1646), the English naturalist Sir Thomas Browne expands on Aelian's notion:

> The common opinion of the *Ostrich, Struthio-camelus* or *Sparrow-camel* conceives that it digesteth Iron; and this is confirmed by the affirmations of many; beside swarms of others, Rhodiginus in his prelections taketh it for granted, Johannes Langius in his Epistles pleadeth experiment for it; the common picture also confirmeth it, which usually describeth this Animal with an horseshoe in its mouth. Notwithstanding upon enquiry we find it very questionable, and the negative seems most reasonably entertained; whose verity indeed we do the rather desire, because hereby we shall relieve our ignorance of one occult quality; for in the list thereof it is accounted, and in that notion imperiously obtruded upon us. For my part, although I have had the sight of this Animal, I have not had the opportunity of its experiment, but have received great occasion of doubt, from learned discourses thereon. . . . Some have experimentally refuted it, as Albertus Magnus; and most plainly Ulysses Aldrovandus, whose words are these: *Ego ferri frusta devorare, dum Tridenti essem, observavi, sed quoe incocta rursus excerneret,* that is, at my being

at Trent, I observed the Ostrich to swallow Iron, but yet to exclude it undigested again.

By medieval times, the naturalists had also given the ostrich another quality: "The ostrich," writes Vincent of Beauvais in his *Specula Naturam,* "has a small bone under its wings which pricks him in the side and stirs the bird to wrath." This was thought to explain the ostrich's notoriously unfriendly attitude toward humans. Not until fairly modern times would descriptions crop up of the ostrich's supposed habit of hiding its head in the sand, thus making itself invisible to predators.

The Bushmen ascribed to the ostrich amazing regenerative abilities, as this story of the resurrection of an Ur-ostrich relates:

The Bushman kills an Ostrich at the Ostrich's eggs; he carries away the Ostrich to the house. And his wife takes off the Ostrich's short feathers which were inside the net, because they were bloody; she goes to place them on the bushes. They eat the Ostrich meat.

A little whirlwind comes to them; it blows up the Ostrich feathers. A little Ostrich feather that has blood upon it, it blows up the little feather into the sky. The little feather falls down out of the sky, it having whirled around, falls down, it goes into the water, it becomes wet in the water, it is conscious, it lies in the water, it becomes Ostrich flesh; it gets feathers, it puts on its wings, it gets its legs, while it lies in the water.

It walks out of the water, it basks in the sun upon the water's edge, because it is still a young Ostrich. Its feathers are young feathers, because its feathers are little feathers. They are black, for a little male Ostrich it is. He dries his feathers lying upon the water's bank, that he may afterwards walk away, when his little feathers are dried, that he may walk unstiffening his legs. For he had been in the water, that he may walk strengthening his feet. While he walks strengthening his feet, he lies down, he hardens his breast, that his breastbone may become bone. He walks away, he eats young bushes, because a young Ostrich he is. He swallows young plants which are small, because a little Ostrich he is. His little feather it was which became the Ostrich, it was that which the wind blew up, while the wind was a little whirlwind; he thinks of the place on which he has scratched; he lets himself grow, that he may first be grown, that he may afterwards, lying by the way, go into his house's old place, where he did die lying there, that he may go to scratch in the old house, while he goes to fetch his wives. He will add to the two previous ones another she Ostrich; because he did die, he will marry three Ostrich wives. Because his breastbone is bone, he roars, hardening his ribs, that his ribs may become bone. Then he scratches out a house; he roaring calls the Ostrich wives, that the Ostrich wives may come to him. Therefore he roaring calls, that he may perceive the she Ostriches come to him, and he meets them, that he may run round the females, for he had been dead, he dying left his wives. He will look at his wives' feathers, for his wives' feathers appear to be fine.

The ostrich was also long thought to be a less than doting parent. In the Book of Job, we read of the female, "which leaveth her eggs in the earth, and warmeth them in dust. And forgetteth that the foot may crush them, or that the wild beast may break them"—a reasonable enough supposition inasmuch as the ostrich does in fact nest on the ground.

All this is useful information, now that ostrich farming—and even trading in ostrich futures—is becoming big business throughout the desert Southwest.

Peregrine falcon

A crusader wrote of his time in the Arabian desert:

Of the various habits of the falcon one I admire so much that it is a pleasure for me to write about it. In winter when frosts hold nature in their grip, the falcon saves himself from the inconvenience of the cold by grasping a partridge or duck, all night captive between its talons. But when the warmth of the sun returns in the morning, the falcon allows the bird that has served its purpose to fly away, as if rewarding it with liberty for the fright it suffered during its nocturnal duty. It disdains to pursue it, mindful of its own mobility, even though the frightened victim might appear to be its legitimate prey. Certain people do not admit its nobility, alleging that the falcon realizes that its nocturnal fear has made the bird so thin that it is hardly now a fit breakfast for the fastidious appetite of the falcon. Others declare that it is a conspicuous example of the falcon's nobility, generous pity, and merciful kindness, which shows not only that those in wretchedness should be helped but also that the least service deserves reward.

Although it occupies much the same ecological niche and exhibits much the same behavior, the noble Arabian falcon of which the crusader wrote is not the same as the North American falcon, *Falco peregrinus,* which now seems to be recovering from near-extinction in the deserts of the Southwest thanks to outstanding efforts by conservation biologists. Whether the North American race similarly warms itself with duck or partridge gloves, though, is a question that science has not yet answered.

Phoenix

Do animals imagine that there are worlds in which they are kings, a world in which it is they who shape reality?

Perhaps so. Aesop tells this story:

> A man and a lion were traveling together through forested mountains. To pass the time, they began to boast to each other of their strength and agility. They argued back and forth for many miles, until they came to an abandoned temple with a stone statue before it depicting an athlete strangling a lion.
>
> The man pointed it out and said, "You see! We humans are the strongest creatures on earth."
>
> The lion answered, "A human made this statue. If lions could sculpt, it would tell an entirely different story."

A different story, indeed. But for all the advances our natural sciences have made in the areas of animal cognition and communication, we still do not know enough about animals to know how, and even whether, they imagine.

We know that humans do. Imagination of a sort prompted a drunken Englishman to stand atop an ancient Hohokam mound outside of the prosaically but accurately named hamlet of Pumpkinville and call it Phoenix, noting the fact that the new American city arose from the ashes of the long-gone Hohokam civilization of the prehistoric Southwest. Imagination prompted some ancient Egyptian to stand along the desert shores of the Nile and relate a story of an inexplicable animal, a fabulous, great bird sacred to Helios and, in subsequent retellings, other Mediterranean sun gods. The Greek word *phoenix* means both "bright-colored" and "palm-tree," which poses a bit of a conceptual problem, palm trees being bright enough but incapable of flight save in the stiffest sirocco. The matter may be explained by the odd fact that the hieroglyph for the ancient Egyptian word *bennu,* meaning a kind of stork, was also that of the homonymic *bennu,* or palm tree, and both terms were applied to the purple heron (*Ardea purpurea*).

In any event, the phoenix was a male bird, the only one of its kind, of magnificent plumage, who lived for an unaccountably long time; the Roman historian Tacitus tells us its life span was 1,461 years, whereas other sources accord it a life of up to 12,954 years. At the end of its life, the legend continued, the phoenix constructed a nest of cassia twigs in a myrrh tree and set itself on fire. From the ashes of its body and nest arose another phoenix, perfectly formed, and gathered its progenitor's remnants, taking them south to the sacred city of Heliopolis and depositing them there on the altar of the Sun. The phoenix appears briefly in the Bible as a promise of longevity: "I shall die in my nest, and I shall multiply my days as the phoenix" (Job 29:18).

The Greeks held that the phoenix was strictly a bird of Egypt, although the Egyptians themselves said that the bird was a native of, variously, Arabia, Mesopotamia, or India, where it appears as the roc or rukh. Farid Ud-Din Attar, who was born about A.D. 1120 in Neishapour, a desert city in what is now northeastern Iran, wrote of the phoenix in his *Manteq at-Tair* (Conference of the Birds), an allegorical rendering of the tenets of Sufism. That pre-Islamic religion of Persia and India was later given sectarian status under Islam, but in his time Farid's poems would earn him banishment from his homeland on the grounds of heresy. He transposes the ancient Egyptian and Greek stories of the fabulous phoenix to the Thar Desert of India:

> *In India lives a solitary bird.*
> *The beautiful phoenix has a long, stiff beak*
> *Full of countless holes, like a flute.*
> *Each hole makes a different sound, and each sound*
> *Is a secret music, deep and hard to comprehend.*
> *And as these mournful notes emerge,*

Every bird around it falls silent,
And even the fish stop to listen. From this
Sad song a wise man once learned music,
And gave it to humans.
The phoenix lives for a thousand years,
And he sees death coming from afar.
Then he builds a pyre of logs
And sings a song of death, and quavers,
And the animals come near to watch,
Some crying in sympathy, some afraid,
Some just to listen.
The phoenix, singing, beats the air,
And fans a roaring fire that soon burns to ash,
And from those ashes a little phoenix rises.
What other creature can first die,
And then give himself birth?
If you lived as long as the phoenix lives,
You would still die some day.
None of us, however crafty,
Can escape death's claws. All of us die;
Not even the phoenix lives forever.
This is the hardest thing
That life puts in our path.

The Anglo-Saxon lay "The Phoenix," nearly contemporane-
ous with Farid's poem, offers a similarly fabulous history while
fantasizing of a land far different from the rock-and-dust desert
that was the phoenix's birthplace:

I have heard that far hence in the east is the noblest of lands,
famous among men. The face of the land is not to be found across
the world by many of earth's dwellers, but by God's might it is
set afar off from evil-doers. Lovely is all the land, covered with
delights, with earth's sweetest scents; matchless is that water-land,
noble its Maker, proud, rich in power; He created the country.
There often to the blessed the delight of harmonies, the door of

heaven is set open and revealed. That is a fair field, green forests spread beneath the skies. There neither rain, nor snow, nor the breath of frost, nor the blast of fire, nor the fall of hail, nor the dropping of rime, nor the heat of the sun, nor unbroken cold, nor warm weather, nor wintry shower shall do any hurt; but the land lies happy and unharmed. That noble land is abloom with flowers. No hills or mountains stand there steeply, nor do stone-cliffs rise aloft, as here with us; nor are there valleys, or dales, or hill-caves, mounds or rising ground; nor are there any rough slopes there at all. But the noble field is fruitful under the sky, blossoming in beauty.

Gentle is that plain of victory; the sunny grove gleams; pleasant is the forest. Fruits fall not, bright are the blooms; but the trees stand ever green as God bade them. Winter and summer alike the forest is hung with fruits; the leaves under the sky shall never wither away, nor the fire ever do them hurt, before a change comes over the world. When long ago the torrent of water, the sea-flood whelmed all the world, the circuit of the earth, then by God's grace the noble field stood secure from the rush of wild waves; no whit harmed, happy, undefiled. Thus it shall bide in blossom till the coming of the fire, the judgment of God, when the graves, the tombs of men, shall be torn open. There is no foe in the land, nor weeping nor woe, nor sign of grief, nor old age, nor sorrow, nor cruel death, nor loss of life, nor the coming of a hateful thing, nor sin, nor strife, nor sad grief, nor the struggle of poverty, nor lack of wealth, nor sorrow, nor sleep, nor heavy illness, nor wintry storm, nor change of weather fierce under the heavens; nor does hard frost with chill icicles beat upon anyone. Neither hail nor rime falls on the ground there; nor is there a windy cloud; nor does water come down there, driven by the gust; but there the streams, wondrously splendid, gush welling forth; they water the land with fair fountains; winsome waters from the midst of the forests, which sprang ocean-cold from the soil, sometimes go gloriously through the whole grove.

A bird wondrous fair, mighty in its wings, which is called the Phoenix, dwells in that wood. Alone there it holds its abode, its brave way of life; never shall death do it hurt in that pleasant place while the world endures. There it is said to gaze on the sun's going and to come face to face with God's candle, the gracious jewel, to watch eagerly till the noblest of heavenly bodies rises gleaming over the waves of the sea from the east, the ancient work of the Father, radiant sign of God, shining in its adornments. The stars are hidden, whelmed under the waves in the west, quenched in the dawn; and the dark night departs with its gloom. Then the bird, mighty in flight, proud of its pinions, gazes eagerly at the ocean, across the waters under the sky, till the light of the firmament comes gliding up from the east over the vast sea.

So the noble bird in its changeless beauty by the water-spring dwells by the surging streams. There the glorious creature bathes twelve times in the brook before the coming of the beacon, heaven's candle; and even as many times, at every bath, cold as the sea, it tastes the pleasant waters of the spring. Then after its sport in the water it rises proudly to a lofty tree, whence most easily it can see the movement in the east when the taper of the sky, the gleaming light, shines clearly over the tossing waters.

As soon as the sun towers high over the salt streams the grey bird goes in its brightness from the tree in the grove; swift in its wings, it flies aloft, pours forth harmony and song to the sky. Then so fair is the way of the bird, its heart uplifted, exulting in gladness, it sings a varied song with clear voice more wondrously than ever a son of man heard under the heavens since the mighty King, the Creator of glory, established the world, heaven and earth. The harmony of that song is sweeter and fairer than all music, and more pleasant than any melody. Neither trumpets, nor horns, nor the sound of the harp, nor the voice of any man on earth, nor the peal of the organ, nor the sweetness of song, nor the swan's plumage, nor any of the delights which God hath devised to gladden men in this dreary world can equal that outpouring. Thus it sings and chants, blissfully glad, till the sun has sunk in the southern sky. Then it is silent and falls to listening; it lifts up its head, bold, sage in thought; and thrice it shakes it feathers swift in flight; the bird is mute.

William Shakespeare may have had this description, or one very similar to it, close to hand when he wrote in *The Tempest,*

Now I will believe . . . that in Arabia
There is one tree, the Phoenix's throne, one Phoenix
At this time reigning there.

Robert Graves, the controversial mythographer, believed that the phoenix, with the chimera and the unicorn, was originally a pictographic representation of a constellation. Eventually, he continued, the pictogram came to be misunderstood as the representation of a living creature. Given the putative behavior of the phoenix, burning in fire and cavorting in sky and water, this celestial explanation makes sense, even if it does rob us of some of the world's mystery.

Prairie dog

Lying adjacent to several mountain-island systems of the Sonoran Desert are fertile grasslands, which intergrade with the plants of the true desert at about four thousand feet above sea level. These and other grasslands have been of signal importance in the development of human civilization; much of the world's food supply comes from domesticated grasses like wheat, corn, barley, millet, and rice. Many other species have long depended on grasslands for their sustenance, too. One is the horse, an ancestor of which, *Nannippus*, developed in the Sonoran Desert nearly four and a half million years ago; bones from this tiny forerunner of the modern *Equus* occasionally crop up in exposed cutbanks and arroyos.

The grasslands of the Sonoran Desert once teemed with one of nature's most gregarious animals, the black-tailed prairie dog

(*Cynomys ludovicianus*), whose underground colonies often shelter hundreds of individuals. Their burrows are a marvel of engineering; at once they help distribute oxygen to tightly compacted soils, helping maintain a healthy layer of vegetation, and they provide a roof for many animals—not only prairie dogs, but also wolf spiders, burrowing owls, rattlesnakes, salamanders, turtles, skunks, badgers, and other species that have adapted to the desert's heat by finding cool comfort underground. These animals collectively demonstrate a natural ethic that humans in these troubled times might profit from studying: it is possible, they show us, that different species can live side by side without either helping or harming each other.

In the folklore of the American West, prairie dogs are said to burrow to underground water sources. The result, when this folklore first became current in the nineteenth century, was the destruction of many colonies as settlers drilled through them in search of elusive water, usually without success.

Rattlesnake

According to the Hohokam creation legend, at the beginning of time Elder Brother, the creator god, made Rattlesnake with detachable teeth, so that human children could play with him freely. The children, however, made constant noise while they played, so that Elder Brother could not sleep. Finally he supplied Rattlesnake with permanent teeth, saying, "Now I have done this for you, and when anything comes near you, you must bite it and kill it. From now on people will be afraid of you. You will not have a friend and will always crawl modestly along."

Charles Darwin observes that the rattlesnake, the only venomous snake that issues an audible warning before striking, would no more give warning to its intended target than a housecat would tell a mouse it was about to devour it. He remarks instead that the rattle acts something like the hood of a cobra or the raised hackles of a dog, as a signal to go away and leave its owner alone. Snakes being generally timid and nonaggressive creatures, his explanation makes good sense, but it is not widely shared, and even today in parts of the Southwest you will hear that a snake's rattles—which are vigorously collected for the tourist market—will go on shaking until sunset once separated from the body. The rattler's spinal column is indeed a durable creation, but it has no powers to sustain life without the heart and other organs.

If you are able without bad consequence to examine the underside of a rattlesnake, do so. There you will find a pair of hard protuberances lying flush to its scales. These are vestigial

toenails, signs that rattlers are related to lizards and shed their
feet somewhere along the evolutionary ladder.

But beware the bite, always. One bit of folklore that has basis
in scientific fact is that the bite of a young rattler is more toxic
than that of an older one. As is the case with so many animal
species, the younger creatures lack self-control, and so their
bites are full of venom. Older rattlers, it would appear, have a
greater sense of what is appropriate, adjusting the venom to the
task at hand.

In all this it is well worth remembering, however, that more
people die of lightning strikes than snakebite every year. And it
is thus strangely natural that desert peoples should long have
equated snakes with lightning and water. The Wuturu hold that
the carpet snake (*Python variegatus*) owns the water of the Aus-

tralian desert, and the traditional O'odham believe that every water source has a serpent-god, a *corúa,* to watch over it. The O'odham water-snake connection is an ancient one, and its origins appear to be Mesoamerican: the Uto-Aztecan linguistic element *co* means snake, and it turns up in the name of the Aztec plumed serpent-god of the east, Quetzalcoatl. In O'odham belief these protector serpents were not aggressive, although they were endowed with huge fangs, and in any contact with humans the *corúas* usually lost. In the event of a serpent-god's death, the O'odham held, its associated spring would dry up, and perhaps the idea of such a vulnerable if fearsome-looking snake kept the desert people from tampering with precious water sources. (The Mexican story of La Llorona, a weeping ghost who wanders along riverbeds and steals children who come too near, has a similar function.) Not all water serpents lived underground, however. Some dwelled in the hearts of the boiling summer thunderstorms that bring rain to the desert, not in life-replenishing droplets but in great black undulating curtains of water, leaving floods and destruction in their wake. It was no sin to kill such serpents, but even the most resourceful Tohono O'odham shaman was no match for the *corúas* of the air.

Here is a song sung by the Djambarbingu people of Arnhem Land:

> *The tongues of the Lightning Snakes flicker and twist,*
> * one to the other ...*
> *Flashing among the cabbage palm foliage ...*
> *Lightning flashing through clouds, flickering tongue of*
> * the Snake ...*
> *Always there, at the wide expanse of water, at the place*
> * of the sacred tree ...*
> *Flashing above the people of the western clans,*
> *All over the sky their tongues flicker, above the Place of*
> * the Rising*

Clouds, the Place of the Standing Clouds,
All over the sky, tongues flickering, twisting ...
Always there, at the camp by the wide expanse of water ...
All over the sky their tongues flicker: at the place of the
    Two Sisters,
    the place of the Wawalag.
Lightning flashing through clouds, flickering tongue of
    the Lightning Snake
Its blinding flash lights up the cabbage palm foliage ...
Gleams on the cabbage palms, and their shining leaves ...

In his treatise on animals, Aelian writes that in India and Libya
the people believed that a snake who killed a human could no
longer descend and creep into its own home, but had to live as
an outcast, "a vagabond and wanderer, living in distress beneath
the open sky throughout summer and winter." This, Aelian
understood, was the gods' punishment for manslaughter, punishment that applied to humans and animals alike.

And from the deserts of India, too, came ancient reports of a
serpent seventy cubits—that is, more than a hundred feet—long.
This serpent once attacked Alexander the Great's invading
Macedonian army. Alexander did not succeed in slaying the serpent, although he is said to have come near enough to it to see
that its eyes were as big as his shield.

Reem

Of the animal known in Biblical times as the reem (Psalms
22:21) we know little, save that it may have been related to
another ancestral and now-extinct bovine, the aurochs. An
ancient Canaanite text adverts to the creature:

On them are horns like bulls,
And humps like buffaloes,
And on them is the face of Baal.

In Hebrew myth the reem exists only a pair at a time, repro-
ducing in seventy-year cycles and then dying, the female killing
the male and then herself dying after giving birth to twins. The
reem may have provided the inspiration for the minotaur of
Greek mythology, and apocryphal Hebrew texts relate a story
of the child David battling a male reem as big as a mountain.
Noah, those texts continue, could not make room in the ark for
so huge a creature, and so he bound the pair of reems to the
stern and let them swim behind, their enormous horns tracing
a rift in the desert earth that can be seen near the city of Tiberias.

Roadrunner

In 1827, Paolo Emilio Botta, an Italian acting as a scout for
French investors in the Far West, sent his family a specimen of
Geococcyx californianus, "a running bird to which is attributed
the ability to kill snakes for food. It has a long tail which it raises
to an almost perpendicular position. It seldom flies but runs
almost as fast as a horse." Botta, as Joseph Kastner points out in
his study of pioneering naturalists, *A Species of Eternity*, is not
remembered in the annals of science for this charming, and
accurate, description, but for discovering some years later the
ruins of the Mesopotamian city of Nineveh and the fabled
palace of the Assyrian tyrant Sargon.

The O'odham knew the roadrunner much more intimately
than did Botta, and to him they assigned the job of mapping out
their territory. Roadrunner, *Tadai*, raced about this way and

that, looking for the boundaries of earth and water and showing the people where to live.

Aficionados of the roadrunner are invited to see the entry for
Coyote, to which, thanks to the ministrations of the brilliant
Chuck Jones, the carnivorous and often bad-tempered bird will
forever be tied.

Scorpion

 The constellation named for him may harbor some of the brightest stars in the night sky, but the Greek hero-god Orion is a figure about whom we know strangely little.

He was, it seems, a local deity of the semidesert provinces of Ionia, and gods of like description were found throughout ancient Arabia and Mesopotamia. He was inducted as a supporting player into the pantheon of the Indo-European invaders when they arrived in Greece three millennia ago. (Pausanias says that there was only one small temple devoted to him in all Greece, in the Boiotian town of Tanagra.) His name means "rain-bringer," a good desert epithet, and in the *Meteorology* Aristotle explains that the rising and setting of Orion signals the beginning and end of the rainy season, times that "are considered to be treacherous and stormy," like Orion himself.

Out of the tangled complex of the four sometimes contradictory myths relating to Orion, far separate from one another in time and space, we can cobble a story that goes something like this:

> The bear-hunter Orion was the tallest and most handsome of the giants born to Euryale and the sea-god Poseidon, stronger and fairer than even the mighty Otos and Ephialtes, his half-brothers, who tried to pile the mountains Ossa upon Pelion so as to storm the heavens themselves. Orion married well; unfortunately, his wife Side incautiously boasted that she was more beautiful than Hera the goddess of heaven, and Hera cast her into the pit of Tartarus to ponder her vanity.

Alone, Orion went to the island of Chios at the invitation of its king Oenopion, "wine-face," a son of Dionysus, who asked Orion to purge the island of its wild beasts in return for his beautiful daughter Merope. For every skin that Orion brought to him, however, Oenopion insisted that there were a dozen more lions, bears, and wolves hiding in the hills, and Orion's task seemed never to end.

Impatient to claim her, Orion raped Merope. Oenopion pretended to let the crime pass, but one night he encouraged Orion to drink freely as much of the wine of Chios as he cared to. When Orion fell into a sodden sleep, Oenopion cut his eyes out and cast him away on the beach.

In due time Helios, the god of the sun, restored Orion's sight to him, and Orion went seeking Oenopion to avenge himself. Oenopion had hidden in a deep cave, and, not finding him on Chios, Orion went off to the palace of Minos on Crete, thinking that Minos might there have sheltered Oenopion—his grandson, as it happens. Oenopion never turned up, and Orion spent his days hunting on Mount Ida.

Aurora, the goddess of the dawn, saw him there and fell in love with him, kidnapping him and taking him into the heavens to be her husband. But Orion, ever the hunter, tried to rape the beargoddess Artemis's attendants, the Pleiades, and Artemis set Skorpio, the scorpion, on Orion to exact retribution.

Skorpio stung Orion as he slept. Both died, and both became constellations, Skorpio always pursuing The Hunter in the night sky.

But first Orion's soul went to the Isles of the Dead, where, Homer says, Odysseus saw him "driving lynxes and lions and other wild beasts across fields of greening asphodel, hunting the animals that he had killed in the desolate mountains in life, his unbreakable iron club in his hand." Orion's favorite hunting dog, Sirius, joined him in the heavens. So, too, did his daughters Menippe and Metioche, sacrificed by the Boiotians to rid their country of plague. Eridanus, the great winding river of the heavens, flows from his heel, for, being Poseidon's son, Orion could walk on water. All of them wheel around the Aurochs (Taurus) and the Great Bear (Ursa Major), whom Orion chased on Earth.

In a surviving fragment of his treatise on astronomy, Hesiod remarks that Orion had once threatened to kill every animal on Earth, reason enough for the gods to stay his bloodsoaked hand and set him high in the night sky, where he could do no harm.

Whether the scorpion said anything to Orion we cannot say, but some varieties of scorpion do, in moments of heightened emotion, emit sound—sound that may in turn heighten emotion in anyone who happens to be around to hear it. Jean Henri Fabre, the great entomologist, also reports that scorpions have a few terrifying habits. He had placed a female and male together in a glass cage, and went to inspect the results the next day:

> Next morning, we found the Scorpioness under the potsherd of the previous day. The little male is by her side, but slain, and more or less devoured. He lacks the head, the claw, a pair of legs. I place the corpse in the open, on the threshold of the home. All day long, the recluse does not touch it. When night returns she goes out and, meeting the deceased on her passage, carries him off to a distance to give him a decent funeral, that is to finish eating him.
>
> This act of cannibalism agrees with what the open-air colony showed me the previous year. From time to time I would find, under the stones, a pot-bellied female making a comfortable ritual meal of her companion of the night. I suspected that the male, if he did not break loose in time, once his functions were fulfilled, was devoured, wholly or partly, according to the matron's appetite. I now have the certain proof before my eyes. Yesterday, I saw the couple enter their home after their usual preliminary, the stroll; and, this morning, under the same tile, at the moment of my visit, the bride is consuming her mate.
>
> Well, one supposes that the poor wretch has attained his ends. Were he still necessary to the race, he would not be eaten yet. The

couple before us have therefore been quick about the business, whereas I see that others fail to finish after provocations and contemplations exceeding in duration the time which it takes the hour-hand to go twice around the clock. Circumstances impossible to state with precision—the condition of the atmosphere, perhaps, the electric tension, the temperature, the individual ardor of the couple—to a large extent accelerate or delay the finale of the pairing.

Aristotle reports that in the desert between Susa and Media, in Persia, every rock harbored a huge scorpion—evidently silent, though whether female or a fortunately escaped male we do not know. For this reason, Aristotle continues, the king of the Persians ordered that, three days in advance of any journey he wished to undertake, his advance guards hunt them down, and he bestowed rich presents on the retainer who brought him the most scorpion carcasses. In Libya, in the meanwhile, the scorpions were said to feed upon snakes, lizards, beetles, and cockroaches, and that anyone who stepped on the dung of those scorpions instantly developed ulcers. Adds Pliny, "It is thought good ... to lay to the sore the very scorpion that caused harm [by biting the victim], or to eat him roasted, and last of all to drink it in two cups of black wine."

Aelian observed, correctly, that the scorpion is viviparous, but he attributed birth not to mating but to spontaneous generation caused by the heat of the desert floor.

In more recent times, the English dramatists Beaumont and Fletcher enshrine the scorpion alongside other supposedly noxious creatures in *Philaster,* their plea for deliverance from females. Perhaps they had divined the behavior that Fabre observed.

> *Let me love lightning, let me be embraced*
> *And kissed by scorpions, or adore the eyes*
> *Of basilisks rather than trust the tongues*
> *Of hell-bred women.*

Sidewinder

There is a great deal of geometrical neatness and nicety, in the sinuous motion of snakes, and other serpents. For the assisting in which action, the annular scales under their body are very remarkable, lying across the belly, contrary to what those in the back, and the rest of the body do; also as the edges of the foremost scales lie over the edges of their following scales, from head to tail, so those edges run out a little beyond, or over their following scales, so as that when each scale is drawn back, or set a little upright, by its muscle, the outer edge thereof, or foot it may be called, is raised also a little from the body, to lay hold on the earth, and so promote and facilitate the serpent's motion. This is what may be easily seen in the slough, or belly of the serpent-kind. But there is another admirable piece of mechanism, that my antipathy to those animals hath prevented my prying into; and that is, that every scale hath a distinct muscle, one end of which is tacked to the middle of its scale; the other, to the upper edge of its following scale.

The wise author of nature, having denied feet and claws to enable snakes to creep and climb, hath made them amends in a way more commodious for their state of life, by the broad skin along each side of the belly, and the undulating motion observable there. By this latter it is they creep; by the former, assisted with the glutinous slime emitted from the snake's body, they adhere firmly and securely to all kinds of superficies, partly by the tenacity of their slime, and partly by the pressure of the atmosphere.

Thus the English naturalist William Derham, in his *Physicotheology* (1713), one of the first near-modern scientific treatises to study seriously the odd means by which snakes move themselves from Point A to Point B.

Herodotus reports that in the desert of Syria near the Euphrates River breeds an especially vicious kind of sidewinder that is a special menace to anyone born outside the region;

humans from the area are safe from them, but anyone else is punished by instant death. Aelian adds that those snakes, when coupling, emit the foulest odor known to humankind.

The whip snake of the Southwest, a demonized version of the sidewinder (*Crotalus cerastes*), itself a smallish rattlesnake, enjoys a peculiar place in local mythology: the whip snake outruns a fleeing victim, wraps itself around the unfortunate person's leg, and whips him to death. Another variant is the legendary hoop snake, an avatar of the amphisbaena of medieval bestiary fame, which supposedly can put its tail in its mouth and roll faster than the fleetest horse can run, and which one itinerant preacher insisted was a beast of the apocalypse, with "tails like unto scorpions, and there were stings in their tails" (Rev. 9:10).

A Spanish explorer in Patagonia—we never learn his name in the official report in which he is quoted—insisted that he had discovered a gigantic kind of sidewinder, saying that he and an Indian guide had happened upon it in the sand and killed it after a long battle. The ten-meter-long *liboya* took its toll, however; the Indian, he said, died of fright at the death of the magically powerful snake.

Late in February 1996, a gardener happened upon a newborn two-headed herald snake in his semidesert plot in eastern South Africa and took it away to the Durban zoo. His discovery came just a few days after severe flash flooding had killed more than a hundred KwaZulu villagers, and on learning of it a KwaZulu representative went to the zoo to demand that the snake, which he supposed to be an avatar of the misery-inflicting, seven-headed *inkanyamba* of ancient myth, be turned over to the tribe for ceremonial execution. Other KwaZulu were not as sure of the snake's ancestry. Said one, "No one can keep an *inkanyamba*," reasoning that the gardener would have been struck dead immediately by the snake's mother on first touching the newborn.

Sphinx moth

Ecology, the science of the relationships between organisms and their world, is about connectedness. In thinking about how connections are forged and maintained in the world, it is possible to go too far. We have as evidence the case of a German scientist who mused, in the 1930s, over why England, a tiny island nation, should be so great a world power. (This was a time, of course, when the tiny nation of Germany sought itself to be a world power.) England's supremacy must be due, the good ecologist noted, to the island's cats, which kill mice, rodents that in turn feed on bumblebee larvae; and because bees are the most efficient pollinators of red clover, on which British cattle feed and thus provide sustenance for the soldiers and sailors of the Empire, well, then, the ecologist concluded, of course the success of England rests on the performance of its feline denizens: QED.

Connections so tenuous sometimes apply in the world, however, as in the case of the saguaro cactus of the Sonoran Desert. Now, by any measure *Cereus giganteus* is an oddball of a plant. Although saguaros have been in the fiercely arid Sonoran uplands for eons, they do not really belong in the desert at all. Instead, they evolved in the tropics, migrating northward at a time when the present Sonoran Desert had a climate more like Jamaica's than Death Valley's.

Ten thousand years ago the region, which runs roughly from just north of Alamos, Sonora, to the lowlands below the Mogollon Rim of Arizona and New Mexico, began to dry up. Inland seas became playas, narrow streams replaced broad rivers, and water-loving cacti like the saguaro were left high and dry. In time they adapted to the new conditions, hoarding water for use in times of drought—and a mature adult can store nine tons of water against just such eventualities.

Unlike many desert plants, too, saguaros can live to a ripe old age. A thirty-year-old cactus will be only a yard high, but when it hits saguaro adolescence it begins to grow more quickly; by the time it has doubled its age it will have quintupled its height, and a few years later it will begin to sprout arms. A forty-foot-tall specimen may be anywhere from 150 to 200 years old, born before Anglos settled in the Southwest.

The first Europeans to arrive in the Sonoran Desert had little use for the saguaro. One of them, the Jesuit priest Ignaz Pfefferkorn, summarized the newcomers' attitude: "The plant," he wrote, "is valuable only for its fine fruit, for otherwise, despite its size and thickness, it is a soft stuff, unfit for any conceivable use." Many of the Anglos who followed had much the same regard for *Cereus giganteus*. In the 1880s, Texas ranchers moved from the shortgrass prairies into the saguaro's domain. By 1890, as many as two million head of cattle were munching their way across the Sonoran Desert, eating whatever plants they happened upon. Saguaro pups—you'll find them under the harboring shelter of grass and mesquite, not far from their parents—were a favorite treat, and across the landscape only mature saguaros soon stood, their descendants somewhere in the ruminants' four stomachs. Because the ranchers had a habit of shooting every coyote and wolf they came across, too, the rodent population in the desert exploded; packrats and jackrabbits finished off whatever pups the cattle had overlooked.

The rise of industrial agriculture made matters worse still. Beginning in the 1910s, farmers in Arizona and Sonora were clearing huge tracts of land for cash crops like cotton and winter vegetables, and millions of saguaros were forever scraped from the soil. And not only that: one of the saguaro's main pollinators is a graceful little insect called the white-lined sphinx moth (*Hyles lineata*), which thrives in moist, irrigated fields.

From those farmlands it carries pesticides to the saguaro, chemicals that cause the cactus to abort its fruit. Remove the sphinx moth and the saguaro naturally declines, and *Hyles lineata* is in increasingly short supply.

Things grow worse still. When cities like Phoenix and Tucson began to mushroom after the Second World War, more cacti went under the bulldozer's blade. The places developers especially love to coat with houses, the gradual slopes that fan out from mountain ranges, are the plant's favorite habitat. In the contest between foothills suburbanization and natural preservation, *Cereus* lost.

The new Sunbelt cities had to be landscaped. Enter cactus rustlers, who brought mature saguaros in from the boondocks to grace recently bladed lots, not only in the Sonoran Desert but also in alien environments like Las Vegas and Los Angeles. Demand continued to grow, with private collectors as far away as Europe and Australia seeking specimens.

Cactus rustling remains a growth industry. For the most part, it's as safe a business as white-collar crime. When one giant saguaro called Old Granddad, stolen from a hillside outside Quartzsite, Arizona, in the winter of 1986, was recovered in a Nevada nursery, the two rustlers received a slap on the wrist. One served only six months of a two-year sentence, and both were fined $250 apiece. And Old Granddad died from transplant shock.

Finally, there's the yahoo factor to consider. Its most famous recent manifestation came on February 4, 1982, when young David Grundman went out with his roommate to Lake Pleasant, north of Phoenix, to indulge in a favorite Arizona pastime: drinking a stream of beer while discharging firearms in the desert. One of his targets happened to be a twenty-six-foot-tall saguaro from which he was standing somewhat short of twenty-six feet away. The bullet-riddled cactus fell on Grundman, killing him almost instantly and proving that instant karma, indeed, is gonna get you. For his troubles, Grundman is memorialized in "Saguaro," a tune by The Austin Lounge Lizards, a full-tilt (and fully twisted) bluegrass band. "Noxious little twerp" is one of the nicer things the group says about him.

Multiple causes contributed to the same effect. In the 1930s the newly created Saguaro National Monument was nationally promoted as the world's greatest "cactus forest," populated by tall, multiple-armed saguaros numbering in the low millions. By 1985 much of the forest had disappeared. The intervening half century had been punctuated by a quiet but steady scientific debate over who, or what, was to blame—and what to do about it—with no end to the demise of *Cereus giganteus* in sight, short, perhaps, of a massive infusion of laboratory-bred white-winged sphinx moths and a ban on pesticides everywhere in the Sonoran Desert.

Tarantula

There be four things which are little upon the earth, but they are exceeding wise:
    The ants are a people not strong, yet they prepare their meat in summer;
    The conies are but a feeble folk, yet they make their houses in the rocks;
    The locusts have no king, yet they go forth all of them by bands;
    The spider taketh hold with her hands, and is in kings' palaces.

                    Proverbs 34:28

The tarantula takes its name from the pleasant southern Italian town of Taranto, an ancient Greek colony that retained the customs of Magna Graecia until modern times. Taranto was a center of the ancient Eleusinian mysteries, ritual performances of "things heard, things said, and things seen," mysteries outlawed and driven underground with the advent of official Christianity. Medieval belief had it that anyone bitten by a tarantula would fall victim to "tarantism," a condition characterized first by lethargy and depression and then, if music were played, by mad dancing that ended only when the victim had dropped dead from exertion; as George Herbert writes in his poem "Doomsday,"

> *Dust, alas! no music feels*
> *But thy trumpet; then it kneels,*
> *As peculiar notes and strains*
> *Cure tarantula's raging pains.*

There is no physiological basis for this belief, for the bite of the tarantula is no fiercer than that of any other large spider, akin to a lingering bee sting. Still, when the Spanish conquistador Gonzalo Fernández de Oviedo y Valdés described seeing in the Mexican desert "spiders of a marveylous biggenesse, their body as bigge as a sparrow," his audience feared the worst, and tarantulas have been hunted ever since, either as kills or as objects for collectors' jars.

Among some tribes of Mexico the tarantula is considered a delicacy. It is said to taste, of course, like chicken.

Termite

According to the Hohokam creation cycle, the termite was the first creature Elder Brother, the creator god, made.

Given the importance of the termite in desert ecology, this is not a bad guess at the great chain of being. Another comes from the South African ecologist Eugene Marais, a longtime student of the social animals, who concluded that a termite hill was a single organism whose inhabitants were individually unimportant, so many cells to be sloughed off when the time came. The mind of the whole subsumed that of its parts, and what Marais called phyletic memory determined how each life would be lived to the higher good of the whole. Baboons, he remarked by contrast, developed individual memories, and those memories formed those of the troop, the tribe, and made the basis of a many-parted culture. Marais's follower Alison Jolly elaborated on the differences between the insect and the human mind: "Our primate ancestors took the path of learning, buffering themselves against the vagaries of the environment by the complexities of their society and their intelligence. We exchanged instinctive certainty for adaptive complexity, and in our myth bought knowledge at the price of innocence."

Vulture

Oh bury me not on the lone prairie
In a narrow grave just six by three,
Where the buzzard waits and the wind blows free,
Then bury me not on the lone prairie.

"The Dying Cowboy"

Vultures, the "indignant desert birds" of William Butler Yeats's great poem "The Second Coming," are to all appearances creatures of leisure. They prefer gliding on a bumpy desert thermal to flying under their own power; they'd rather hunker down to a found meal than hunt for themselves. The ones you'll see perching atop Arizona's power lines and cliff edges seem almost to be caricatures, emblems of easy living. But on this bright early-March dawn, the turkey vulture perched just across the slender Bill Williams River from me had taken leisure to unusually laid-back extremes. Far from flying off in alarm at my approach, as just about any other bird would, this specimen of *Cathartes aura* greeted me with the avian equivalent of a yawn.

The turkey vulture's nonchalance made me wonder whether it had ever encountered humans before. There was good reason to suspect that it had not. The Bill Williams is easily Arizona's remotest, least-visited river, lying far from paved roads anywhere but at its beginning in west-central Arizona and its end at the Colorado River between Parker and Lake Havasu City in the fast-growing Mojave Valley. Only a handful of people know the Bill Williams well, and to the flood of Arizona literature the river has contributed just a few drops. It took me nearly two decades' worth of collecting Arizona's wild places before I stumbled across it myself, finally filling in an uncharted quadrant of my personal map of exploration.

Humans, I suspected, were an equally rare find for its wild denizens, like the turkey vulture, to whom Henry David Thoreau adverted when he observed, "We need to witness our own limits transgressed, and some life pasturing freely where we never wander. We are cheered when we observe the vulture feeding on the carrion which disgusts and disheartens us and deriving health and strength from the repast." Perhaps so. Petronius, the Roman poet, was not so cheered, remarking, "The vulture which explores our inmost nerves is not the bird of whom our dainty poets talk, but those evils of the soul, envy and excess."

In Aztec myth, the turkey vulture shares a lineage with humans:

> A long time ago a man who tired of working every day sat down on a stone and studied a passing vulture. "That vulture just flies around all day," he said, "and does nothing. I wish I could be like him." Then he called the vulture and said, "I want to turn into a vulture like you. I'm tired of all this hard work." The vulture said, "Very well. But listen. If you want to eat, you have to eat the things I do. I can't eat tortillas like you. All I can eat is dead things like chickens and dogs. If you can eat those things you can become like me." The man said, "Well, I can eat just about anything." So he jumped high into the air and changed places with the vulture. But after a while he got tired of flying around and eating dead things, and he thought it might even be good to work his fields once again. Still, he had changed into a vulture, and he could not change back.

Without the vulture, many earthbound scavengers would not be able to locate food as quickly as they do. The quick vulture comes in to feed—incidentally, only the turkey vulture and greater and lesser yellow-headed vultures are guided to carrion by smell—and hyenas, jackals, and coyotes follow to clean up afterward, the vulture having tipped them off.

In their book *Innocent Killers* Jane Goodall and Hugo van Lawick recount the wildebeest calving season, when hundreds of newborn wildebeests and their surrounding placentas dot the Serengeti plain. Vultures would first plummet from the sky to gather what they could, while the jackals and hyenas, just as soon as they could ascertain which direction the birds were flying in, "streaked across the open plain, often arriving only seconds after the vulture itself and getting most of the afterbirth." The vultures seem not to mind, the authors note; they once witnessed a vulture fighting off a martial eagle that was dragging a young silverback jackal skyward to enjoy as a meal.

The O'odham peoples of southern Arizona and northern Mexico historically attributed the origin of diseases to the influence of different animals. To the vulture, unhappily, they assigned the sores that come from tertiary syphilis. Other animals fared no better in O'odham nosology: Gila monsters were held to cause fever, horned toads rheumatism, jackrabbits ulcers, rattlesnakes infections of the kidney and bladder, and butterflies all sorts of gastrointestinal discomforts.

Still, they also credited the vulture with shaping their landscape; the creator god charged Ñu:wi, the first *Cathartes aura*, to fly over the desert and shape the mountains and valleys with his wings, for the completion of which task he was honored with this song:

Buzzard bird, buzzard bird,
You have made the land just right.

Buzzard bird, buzzard bird,
You have made the mountains just right.

And apart from making the land just right, the vulture made the passage into the other world right as well in many ancient cultures. In Çatal Hüyük, Anatolia, more than eight thousand years ago, vultures disposed of the dead; they did so in several cultures in Africa and Tibet as well, although the tradition seems not to have been followed in the Americas. The Greek writer Pollux records that the Caspii, the people of what is now Turkmenistan, played funerary songs on the hollowed-out bones of vultures, and the funerary priests of ancient Egypt occasionally dressed in robes made of vulture feathers.

All that would not have impressed Charles Darwin, who wrote of the vulture, "It is a disgusting bird, with its bald scarlet head formed to wallow in putridity."

Wolf

It has been more than half a century since the mountains and hills of Arizona rang with the howls of the Mexican gray wolf, once the ancient night music of the uplands. Down along the boulder-choked canyon of the Blue River, a narrow stream that runs alongside the New Mexico border about 150 air miles northeast of Tucson, the ululations of *Canis lupus* have been stilled even longer. For the first half of the present century, a combined force of federal, state, and private guns determined to make certain that wolves would be only a memory of untamed times.

That army succeeded. On battlegrounds like the Blue, the Santa Catalina Mountains, and the Canelo Hills they exterminated Arizona's wolves one by one, making the mountains, forests, and grasslands of Arizona and New Mexico safe for low-risk livestock ranching, for a surplus population of sheep and cattle. Few extirpations have been as successful; few have removed a key predator species in so short a time. It's not a record to be proud of.

The federal government once engineered the destruction of the Southwest's native wolves at the behest of a few ranchers. That government is now urging that the Mexican gray wolf be reintroduced into two areas within its former range by the end of 1996. Local livestock producers oppose the notion. So, too, do many environmentalists, although many more would like to see wolves returned. The debate surrounding *lobo* is beginning to produce strange alliances, while at the same time pointing to old divisions and longstanding special interests.

Cui bono? Who gains from bringing an outcast species back into the fold? Firm answers have yet to emerge. What does seem clear—tragically, ironically—is that the Mexican gray wolf, the supposed beneficiary of scientific largess, will suffer once again if the government biologists succeed with their plans.

Conditioned by a European legacy full of tales of rapine wolves, the earliest Anglo settlers in the Southwest expected to find a land teeming with monsters. They had reinforcements in guidebooks like one written in 1850 for travelers along the Gila Trail, which warned, "In traveling through the valleys of this section, you will pass through hundreds of wolves, during the day, which evince no timidity, but with heads and tails down, in their natural crouching manner, they pass within a very few rods of you." The fearless wolf packs never materialized. Most settlers nonetheless did their best to do in any lobos that they happened upon, but the land still afforded plenty of shelter.

In the 1880s, however, cattle began to arrive in large numbers in the Southwest when ranchers like Henry Hooker abandoned the overgrazed plains of West Texas. Those ranchers were determined to make the territory their own, and they were not often given to sharing it with creatures they perceived as harmful to their interests. Badgers dig holes in the ground that can break a wandering cow's leg, hares browse the grasses on which steers fatten, river otters build warrens along streambanks that keep a calf from reaching water: the ready solution was to wipe out the offending animal.

Canis lupus had two things going against it. Not only was it a predator, but it also inhabited just the places where cattlemen wanted to put their herds: the grassy, well-watered uplands. No sooner was industrial ranching introduced into the Southwest

than were producers writing back east to Washington demand-
ing that the federal government use its might to vanquish
wolves—not even saving a few for the reservation, as it had for
other indigenes. In 1897, for instance, a rancher on the San Francisco River, into which the Blue empties, wrote to his congress-
man to complain that wolves were destroying half a million
head of cattle each year in the Gila highlands.

It was an incredible exaggeration, but no matter; it led the
government to establish the first program to destroy predators,
a legacy that remains with us in the form of various animal-
control agencies. A few years later another rancher remarked
before a government board, "If the lobo has any useful qualities or habits, I have not yet learned of them. ... It seems to be
a specialist in carnage and to have brought professional skill to
the slaughter of cattle."

The ranchers found a sympathetic audience in government cir-
cles. William Hornaday, a hunter and writer who, as a friend of
Theodore Roosevelt, had considerable influence in the Department of the Interior, advised his readers: "Of all the wild creatures in North America, none are more despicable than wolves.
There is no depth of meanness, treachery or cruelty to which
they do not cheerfully descend. They are the only animals on
earth which make a regular practice of killing and devouring
their wounded companions, and eating their own dead."

Wolves do no such thing, but no matter. Beginning in World
War I, when beef was at a premium, a combined team of Arizona and New Mexico forest rangers combed the highlands of
the Southwest on the hunt for wolves. Their annual takes are
appalling: in 1916 they killed 85 Mexican gray wolves; in 1918,
111; in 1919, 131. Thanks to a relentless program of shooting
and poisoning with cyanide or strychnine, by 1925 they had
reduced the population of wolves in the Southwest to nearly
nothing. Twenty years later there were no wolves known to live

outside captivity in Arizona, apart from a few strays from Mexico. Gid Graham, a former bounty hunter, sadly recalled the program in New Mexico:

> Bear, wolf, and lion were almost exterminated many years ago. Hordes of high salaried trappers and poisoners were sent forth in every state west of the Mississippi River—to fight wild animals! Millions of small fur-bearers—'possums, skunks, minks, foxes and coyotes were poisoned—many faithful dogs died horribly.
>
> These animals preyed almost exclusively on mice, rats, prairie dogs, and gophers—held them in check. . . .
>
> Bear, wolf and lion are gone. Biological Survey has become a racket. More men on the pay-rolls than ever before, costing taxpayers hundreds of millions of dollars. Farmers, ranchmen and hunters will hold in check the few coyotes left and this B.S. outfit should be abolished—is no longer needed. Write to your members of Congress and demand abolishment of this colossal bureau of political parasites. I am against all men and bureaus that poison small fur-bearers and birds.

By 1950, the combined task force could proudly proclaim, "The fiscal year has passed without a single wolf being recorded by the cooperative hunting force. *This has never happened before.*"

And with that epitaph, thought the ranchers, the matter was finished.

Canis lupus was first federally listed as endangered on March 11, 1967, a status that received greater recognition under federal law when the Endangered Species Act of 1973 was signed into law. It has also been on the Arizona Game and Fish Department list of threatened native wildlife for several years, earning it the additional protection—at least in theory—of state law-enforcement officials. Early on, AGFD scoffed at the notion that the wolf's passing was a done deal; "a few individuals," one agency report noted, "are thought to persist in the wild in Mexico, and perhaps occasionally in southern Arizona."

Miraculously, one such persistent animal, the so-called Aravaipa Wolf, turned up a quarter of a century after the last of its brethren had been seen in the area. Haunting the deep canyons of Aravaipa Creek, a wild area off the San Pedro River northeast of Tucson, the lobo killed a few elderly cattle over the space of a year and a half, enough to drive area ranchers to hire a bounty hunter to track the offending creature down. In 1976, despite its protection under law, the Aravaipa Wolf met its end. The bounty hunter walked away $500.00 richer.

Despite the lack of a free-ranging population to study, scientists have learned a great deal about lobos in the last half century. They now believe, for one thing, that wolves and other large predators make for good herd-tenders. Like the Aravaipa Wolf, these predators normally take out only sick or elderly livestock, thus thinning the population to favor strong animals: natural selection at work. (Even then, notes biologist David Mech, wolves are successful in hunting only seven out of every one hundred attempts.) Without wolves, populations of competing foragers like deer and elk have exploded to near-pest levels, and the state government has repeatedly raised the legal limit on their kills in order to reduce their swelling numbers. As the conservationist Aldo Leopold noted, "A deer herd deprived of wolves and coyotes is more dangerous to wilderness areas than the most piratical senator or the go-gettingest chamber of commerce."

Enter the United States government. Armed with this new—or at least newly recognized—biological information, federal scientists proffered the so-called Mexican Wolf Recovery Plan of 1992, hoping through a program of captive breeding to reintroduce a hundred Mexican wolves to a 5,000-square-mile area within *Canis lupus*'s historic range. Working with state wildlife officials, the U.S. Fish and Wildlife Service identified New Mexico's White Sands Missile Range as the best regional habitat.

Arizona Game and Fish Department officials were ready for their federal counterparts. As early as 1984, notes AGFD threatened-species coordinator Terry Johnson, state biologists had been formulating provisional plans for reintroducing lobo to remote areas in Arizona. Somehow that news made its way to the Arizona Farm Bureau and the Arizona Cattle Grower's Association, whose leaders and members flooded AGFD with letters of protest. The department publicly backed off, but some of its members continued studying the idea, and in February and March of 1990 AGFD surveyed 3,221 Arizonans about their attitudes on reintroduction; 77 percent of those polled favored reintroduction, 13 percent were opposed, and 10 percent had no opinion. (A Montana poll conducted that year showed much the same distribution.)

Those numbers, it appears, changed some minds. In 1991, the Arizona Wool Producers Association publicly announced that its membership would not oppose reintroduction if livestock producers were compensated for any wolf-caused losses. Shortly thereafter the Cattle Grower's Association and the Farm Bureau unaccountably dropped their opposition to reintroduction.

At the beginning of 1992, AGFD released a draft proposal prepared by Terry Johnson to reintroduce wolves into four state wilderness areas, all within a few hours' drive of Tucson. In the nearest, the Atascosa/Patagonia Mountains north of Nogales, the department initially suggested the release of four mating pairs of wolves, with similar numbers projected for the Pinaleño Mountains near Safford, the Chiricahua Mountains of southeastern Arizona, and the Blue River.

The Atascosa/Patagonia Mountains, together offering about 3,840 square miles of prime wolf habitat, were especially attractive. There, biologist Stanley P. Young noted in his famed 1940 study *The Wolves of North America,* lay one of the region's best-defined wolf runways, a runway being, among other things, a path that surrounds a pack's turf. Young estimated that it formed "an irregular circle," and he traced what he called the Canelo Hills run from a point about twenty miles south of Parker Canyon, over the San Rafael Valley to the Canelo Hills, onward over the Patagonia Mountains, and then on to the Mexican border—a distance of about seventy miles.

Many biologists believe that any newly reintroduced wolves would easily adapt to the runway, and that the Atascosa/Patagonia area was ideal. But AGFD eliminated the sector for reintroduction. Terry Johnson would not venture an official explanation, but in the 1992 report he notes that nearly a third of the area is privately owned, mostly by ranchers, so local opposition may have been a factor. So, too, may the fact that the Santa Cruz corridor between Tucson and Nogales is rapidly growing.

AGFD later ruled out as well the 4,499-square-mile Chiricahua Mountains and the 4,183-square-mile Galiuro/Pinaleño region, where the Aravaipa Wolf met its end. Instead, it settled on the Blue Range Primitive Area, a small (1,576-square-mile) but choice piece of territory that boasts a 5,000-foot elevation, a low human population, few roads, and the kind of rocky, broken terrain in which wolves like to make their dens.

By a nice turn, the Blue is also the area where Aldo Leopold, one of the guiding lights of American environmentalism, converted from hunter to ecologist. In the early years of this century Leopold killed dozens of wolves in his work as a forester on the Mogollon Rim, but he came to regret his contribution, however, when he witnessed his handiwork at close range. As he recalled in his famous memoir *A Sand County Almanac,* a shot went astray, and he failed to make what hunters boast of as a "clean kill":

We reached the old wolf in time to watch a fierce green fire dying in her eyes. I realized then and have known ever since that there was something new to me in those eyes—something known only to her and the mountain. I was young then, and full of trigger itch; I thought that because fewer wolves meant more deer, that no wolves would mean hunter's paradise. But after seeing the green fire die, I sensed that neither the wolf nor the mountain agreed with such a view.

Dan Groebner, a wildlife biologist who came to Arizona from Wisconsin to serve as the AGFD wolf-reintroduction coordinator, thinks much the same. He has made several surveying trips along the Blue, and agrees that the area is just right for lobo. He has been pressing his case, and he hopes to hear *Canis lupus* howling along the river within two years. "The timetable for releasing the wolf," he says, "is to have the Environmental Impact Statement completed by the end of this year, then have a public comment period, then a revision of the draft, and then hopefully a completed EIS by the end of 1995. No release is likely before 1996, but I hope it won't be much later than that."

The plan is modest enough on the surface, but plenty big when it comes to real numbers. At last count there were forty-four Mexican gray wolves in captivity in the United States, and perhaps as many in Mexico. (The figures are vague; more individuals may live in captivity under private ownership.) Although wolf packs usually number from six to a dozen animals, they can reach up to twenty. Dan Groebner projects releasing only two to four wolves initially, noting, "The important measure is the number of breeding packs, not how big they are."

Having been bred in captivity, the wolves will not, of course, have any experience in the wild. Groebner plans to feed them roadkilled animals for a period of no more than six weeks, while at the same time teaching the wolves how to hunt for themselves. This is a difficult proposition, he realizes. A few years ago a Canadian rancher named Bill Mason who bred a few pairs of timber wolves decided to release his charges into the wild. When he went into the backcountry to check on the wolves a month later, he found them starving despite the abundance of caribou and deer all around them. They simply had not taught themselves how to feed, and Mason had to return them to their pens. For all that, Groebner remains undaunted.

Asked whether a diet of roadkill will not draw wolves to roads, where they may easily become roadkill themselves, Groebner has no ready reply. Neither is he overly concerned that other wolf-reintroduction programs have ended badly, notably one involving four timber wolves released in the Upper Peninsula of Michigan in 1974. Within nine months three of them had been shot dead by hunters, while the fourth had been run down by an automobile. As the U.S. Fish and Wildlife Service report on the matter noted, in the dry language of professional bureaucrats, "Human-caused mortality was responsible for the failure of the wolves to establish themselves." Groebner believes that educating hunters will prevent the same thing from happening on the Blue.

Canis lupus may ultimately fail to establish there, however. If AGFD moves ahead with its plan, it is certain to face a political fight. Most local ranchers, despite the approval of their statewide association, oppose the plan, and Groebner reports that he is having considerable difficulty persuading them of the merits of reintroduction. Those ranchers have disproportionate pull in the conservative Legislature, and many have already made their feelings known in Phoenix. Only a concerted effort, Groebner admits, will overcome their resistance. As David Mech, North America's greatest living authority on wolves, puts it, "If the wolf is to survive, the wolf haters must be outnumbered. They must be outshouted, outfinanced, and outvoted."

The ranchers, already feeling under siege thanks to Interior Secretary Bruce Babbitt's plan to increase grazing fees on public land, have two chief fears. The first, despite good evidence against it, is that wolves will destroy their herds; they are little impressed by an AGFD contingency fund that will pay fair market value for any livestock they lose. The second is that the wolves will attack humans, killing them outright or infecting them with rabies.

Neither scenario seems likely. According to David Mech, there is no record of wolves ever having killed a person in North America. It is true, he continues, that the only recorded instances of wolves attacking humans have involved rabies, a disease that is on the rise throughout the Southwest. Craig Levy, program manager of the Vector and Zoonotic Disease Section of the Arizona Department of Health, sees little to worry about in the case of wolves, however.

"I'm all for reintroducing the Mexican gray wolf," Levy says. "From a public health standpoint the problems with them are minimal. Skunks, bats, and foxes are the three wild animals we tend to look out for. In Pima, Santa Cruz, and Cochise counties we're seeing a rising phase of skunk rabies, and wolves would of course be susceptible to that. But we usually see maybe one rabid coyote in the state every five years or so; by contrast, we've seen thirteen rabid skunks and six rabid dogs just in the first four months of 1994. Wolves, being more cautious of contact with other creatures, are probably safer than coyotes. They're smart, and they tend to stay away from danger."

There is always the chance, Groebner concedes, that a reintroduced wolf may develop a fondness for beef or mutton; in the past, a few "renegades" like Old Aguila, Three Toes, and the Custer Wolf tore wide swaths through cattle herds throughout the Southwest. But, he says, "If we label the wolves as 'experimental,' then according to federal law we can remove or relocate problem animals." He goes on to say, "The ranchers I've spoken with are very concerned with losing cattle to wolves, but we're trying to work with them. We are definitely going to be sensitive to their concerns."

Like most of her neighbors, Jo Baéza, a White Mountains–based writer and onetime rancher, opposes reintroduction, while still appreciating the work of groups like the White Mountain Conservation League to restore large predators to the high country. "For lots of reasons, people up here are uncomfortable with the idea of wolves being reintroduced on the Blue," she says. "The area is pretty populated now, especially with all the newcomers who have left Southern California for small-town life, and none of the ranchers down on the river wants to see wolves. I don't think the government is going to get this one through."

Another rancher, who did not want to be identified by name, agreed. "Wolves aren't known to be friendly creatures." (In his famous study *The Wolves of Mount McKinley*, Adolph Murie observed, "The strongest impression remaining with me after watching ... wolves on numerous occasions was their friendliness.") The rancher continued, "Of course we're worried about losing our stock. We're also worried about what will happen to our recreation industry. Lots of people hike up here, and they'll go someplace else when the wolves start attacking them.

"I believe that God gave everything a place in nature," the rancher says. "Where the wolf's place is, though, I don't know. It sure isn't here."

David Brown, a retired wildlife biologist and current adjunct professor of biology at Arizona State University, has been studying the Mexican gray wolf for decades. His work has yielded, among other things, his important book *The Wolf in the Southwest*, which is now in its fourth printing. In that book, first published in 1983, Brown suggests that any reintroduction effort is doomed to failure. Eleven years later, he remains skeptical, saying, "I wouldn't change a word of what I wrote."

"I may have softened a little," Brown continues, "but not much. I haven't seen anything concrete to make me alter my opinion. Captive animals have a very bad record of success, whether they be thick-billed parrots, masked bobwhites, bears, or whatever. They can't just be planted like corn. Granted, up on the Blue we probably have sufficient territory to support wolves, but that territory is also full of people who just wouldn't let the wolves alone. In the 1970s, when the Aravaipa Wolf was running down in the Galiuros, a lot of people were trying to gun it down.

"Now," Brown goes on to say, "a wolf that's not raised in the wild is something else. It's not a wolf. Captive wolves learn quickly, to be sure; they learn that bringing down an old cow is easier than chasing down an antelope. I fear that we'll see a lot of wolves in trouble with ranchers. You'll need to set up a large livestock-free area for the wolves, and there just isn't any such place in the Southwest. The reason wolves succeed in Canada and Alaska is that there are few ranchers and plenty of wild game. Down here the situation is the reverse, and the wolves are going to suffer because of it."

Dan Groebner counters, "The evolutionary instincts built into the wolf are very strong. A few generations of captivity won't likely have much of an effect on them. A few things like hunting will have to be learned, and while they're doing that, we'll be supplying them with roadkill and weaning them gradually."

The fact that the stock of wolves is likely to come only from captive animals troubles some environmentalists and biologists. But that may be the only genetic source left. There is now a strong possibility that the wolf has been extinguished even in the remotest corners of the Sierra Madre of Mexico, an area that has long been ranched and that is now undergoing intensive logging and development. Julio Guerrero, a Mexican government biologist who has been looking for wolves in the Sierra Madre for the last decade, reportedly has not seen any signs of *Canis lupus* there in the last three years. Dave Brown remarks, "It would probably be a lot easier to find a grizzly bear than a wolf in Mexico right now. I think they're gone."

Groebner believes that the wolves are still around, however, and in sufficient number to say, "It's always possible that Mexican gray wolves could recolonize the area naturally. There have been a few unconfirmed sightings in southern Arizona, and a few individuals may be coming up on their own."

Jo Baéza also believes that the wolf has not been entirely driven out of its range. "When I lived way out on the Rim, by Deer Springs," she says, "I heard and saw them all the time. They were regular Mexican gray wolves, I'm sure of it. So few people live out in remote areas these days—even the ranchers live in town—that we've probably forgotten that wild country is still pretty wild, and that animals we believe extinct can still be out there. Ask any Apache cowboy. They know where wolf territory is."

Dave Brown is unimpressed. "Yeah," he says, "people see wolves. But then people see the Virgin of Guadalupe all the time, too. People see Jesus in tortillas."

The tangled problem of wolf reintroduction may have only one or two clear-cut solutions. One is draconian: buy out the ranchers through eminent domain, close off roads into the Blue, and let the once-remote region revert to wilderness; discourage any human presence, however well-meaning; patrol the region against yahoo hunters looking for a wolf's head for the living-room wall, impose the death penalty on anyone caught preying on an endangered species, for there are plenty more humans than other large predators. In these days of government cuts, head-long development, and antienvironmentalist backlash, however, such a scenario is unlikely in the extreme.

In any event, the question remains, is reintroducing *Canis lupus* truly to the benefit of the creature itself, or is it for our own aesthetic, the guilt-assuaging dream of urban environmentalists? Is drawing back a species from the dead akin morally to keeping a brain-dead patient alive on a respirator, hoping against hope?

We know too little of the systematic biology of wolves to be sure of their post-captivity adaptability to the wild, but with wilderness everywhere under siege, it may simply not be fair to turn the wolves out until their territory is secure, and far larger than the present fraction of their normal range that is being proposed. For that reason the Humane Society of America opposed the Northern Rocky Mountain Gray Wolf Restoration Act of 1990, siding with the ranchers of Montana and Wyoming against reintroduction but for opposite reasons, saying that the number of wolves (the U.S. Fish and Wildlife Service proposed three mating pairs) was inadequate, the protected territory too limited to be fair to lobo. As the writer Rick Bass points out in his recent book *The Ninemile Wolves*, once extirpated, the wolves stayed out of the United States for a reason: they're smart enough to know where their enemies are.

"Impossible to imagine how dangerous the world will be without animals," Elias Canetti presciently jotted in his World

War II diary. Dangerous indeed. In our time, large-animal species are being daily destroyed. Fewer than five thousand tigers are now thought to exist the world over; elephants, lions, and gorillas are being marched off to extinction by "human-caused mortality." Marian Gierlach, an editor at the Tucson-based *Wildlife Damage Review*, estimates that in 1993 alone more than three hundred mountain lions were killed statewide in the interest of protecting livestock. That number, she continues, represents one-tenth of the entire population of *Felis concolor*.

And the slaughter of wolves continues today in Alaska, where Governor Walter Hickel argues, "You can't just let nature run wild." (Acting as Hickel's interpreter, Alaska Game and Fish officer David Johnson elaborates, "If you slaughter cows, drown rats, or poison mosquitoes, is killing wolves so wrong?") Yes, it is a dangerous world, too dangerous for wolves to be guaranteed safety outside the confines of a cage. Soon it may be too dangerous for us. Only then will the wolf survive.

Bibliography

Ackerman, Diane. *The Moon by Whale Light.* New York: Random House, 1991.

_____. *The Rarest of the Rare.* New York: Random House, 1995.

Aelian. *On the Characteristics of Animals.* Three volumes. Edited by A. F. Schofield. Cambridge: Harvard University Press, 1958.

Allan, J. A., ed. *The Sahara: Ecological Change and Early Economic History.* London: Menas Press, 1978.

Allen, Mary. *Animals in American Literature.* Urbana: University of Illinois Press, 1983.

Angier, Natalie. *The Beauty of the Beastly.* Boston: Houghton Mifflin, 1995.

Aristotle. *Historia Animalia.* Rome: Brettschneiders, 1911.

Babur, Zaruddin Muhammad. *The Baburnama.* Translated by Wheeler M. Thackston. New York: Oxford University Press, 1996.

Bahr, Donald M., Juan Smith, William Smith Allison, and Julian Hayden. *The Short, Swift Time of Gods on Earth: The Hohokam Chronicles.* Berkeley: University of California Press, 1994.

Bent, Arthur Cleveland. *Life Histories of North American Birds.* Twenty volumes. Washington, D.C.: U.S. Government Printing Office, 1937.

Berndt, Ronald M., and Catherine H. Berndt. *The World of the First Australians.* Chicago: University of Chicago Press, 1964.

Bierhorst, John. *Mythology of Mexico and Central America.* New York: Morrow, 1990.

Bleek, W.H.I., and L. C. Lloyd. *Specimens of Bushmen Folklore.* London: George Allen and Co., 1911.

Bonner, John Tyler. *The Evolution of Culture in Animals.* Princeton: Princeton University Press, 1980.

Bowles, Paul. *Their Heads Are Green and Their Hands Are Blue.* New York: Random House, 1963.

Boyer, L. Frank. *Childhood and Folklore.* New York: Library of Psychological Anthropology, 1979.

Bridges, E. Lucas. *Uttermost Part of the Earth.* New York: Dutton, 1949.

Brinton, Daniel. *Ancient Nahuatl Poetry.* Philadelphia: Library of Aboriginal American Literature, 1898.

Brown, Cecil H. *Language and Living Things.* New Brunswick: Rutgers University Press, 1984.

Buchmann, Stephen, and Gary Paul Nabhan. *Forgotten Pollinators.* Washington, D.C.: Island Press, 1996.

Burroughs, Raymond D., ed. *The Natural History of the Lewis and Clark Expedition.* Lansing: Michigan State University Press, 1961.

Burton, R. G. *A Book of Man-Eaters.* Delhi: Mittal Publications, 1984.

Burton, Robert. *Bird Behavior.* New York: Alfred A. Knopf, 1985.

Chadwick, Douglas. *The Fate of the Elephant.* San Francisco: Sierra Club Books, 1993.

Conniff, Richard. "The King of Sting." *Outside,* April 1996.

Darwin, Charles. *The Voyage of the Beagle.* New York: Anchor Books, 1962.

Densmore, Frances. *Papago Music.* Washington, D.C.: U.S. Government Printing Office, 1929.

Downs, Robert B., ed. *The Bear Went Over the Mountain.* New York: Macmillan, 1971.

Ehrlich, Paul R., and Peter H. Raven. "Butterflies and Plants: A Study in Coevolution." *Evolution,* Vol. 18, No. 3 (December 1964): 586–608.

Elton, Charles S. *The Pattern of Animal Communities.* London: Methuen, 1966.

Evers, Larry, and Felipe S. Molina. *Yaqui Deer Songs.* Tucson: University of Arizona Press, 1987.

Foucault, Michel. *The Order of Things.* New York: Random House, 1970.

Franklin, Kevin. "Water Worries." *Tucson Weekly,* March 14, 1996.

Frobenius, Leo. *Volksmärchen und Volksdichtungen Afrikas.* Ten volumes. Jena: Institut für Kulturmorphologie/Eugen Diederichs Verlag, 1921.

Frobenius, Leo, and Douglas C. Fox. *African Genesis.* Berkeley: Turtle Island Foundation, 1983.

Galeano, Eduardo. *Memory of Fire.* Translated by Cedric Belfrage. Three volumes. New York: Pantheon, 1985.

George, Uwe. *In the Deserts of This Earth.* New York: Harcourt Brace Jovanovich, 1976.

Gould, James L., and Carol Grant Gould. *The Animal Mind.* New York: Scientific American, 1994.

Graham, Gid. *Animal Outlaws.* Collinsville, Okla.: privately published, 1938.

Graves, Robert. *The Greek Myths.* Harmondsworth: Penguin Books, 1955.

Griffin, Donald R. *The Question of Animal Awareness.* New York: Rockefeller University Press, 1981.

Heinrich, Bernd. "Of Bedouins, Beetles, and Blooms." *Natural History,* May 1994.

Henschel, Joh. "Spider Revolutions." *Natural History,* March 1995.

Hölldobler, Bert, and Edward O. Wilson. *The Ants.* Cambridge: Harvard University Press, 1990.

Jolly, Alison. *The Evolution of Primate Behavior.* New York: Macmillan, 1972.

Jones, Chuck. *Chuck Amuck.* New York: Farrar, Straus & Giroux, 1989.

Kastner, Joseph. *A Species of Eternity.* New York: Knopf, 1977.

Keast, Allen. *Australia and the Pacific Islands: A Natural History.* London: Hamish Hamilton, 1966.

Klingender, Francis. *Animals in Art and Thought.* Cambridge: MIT Press, 1971.

Kramer, Samuel Noah, ed. *Mythologies of the Ancient World.* New York: Doubleday, 1961.

Lawlor, Robert. *Voices of the First Day: Awakening in the Aboriginal Dreamtime.* Rochester, Vermont: Inner Traditions, 1991.

Lawrence, R. D. *The Green Trees Beyond: A Memoir.* New York: Henry Holt, 1994.

Lenihan, Daniel J. "Ground Zero Revisited." *Natural History,* July 1995.

Lévi-Strauss, Claude. *The Savage Mind.* Chicago: University of Chicago Press, 1966.

Lines, William J. *Taming the Great South Land.* Berkeley: University of California Press, 1991.

Livingston, David. *Missionary Travels and Researches in South Africa.* London: Murray, 1857.

Lorenz, Konrad. *Behind the Mirror: A Search for a Natural History of Human Knowledge.* New York: Harcourt Brace Jovanovich, 1977.

Mabry, Richard, ed. *The Oxford Book of Nature Writing.* New York: Oxford University Press, 1995.

MacMahon, James A. *Deserts.* New York: Knopf, 1985.

Matson, Daniel Shaw. "Papago Recordings." *Arizona Quarterly* Vol. 9, No. 1 (Spring 1953): 45–54.

Matthiessen, Peter. *Wildlife in America.* New York: Viking, 1959.

Mayr, Ernst. *The Growth of Biological Thought.* Cambridge: Harvard University Press, 1982.

McNamee, Gregory. *Gila: The Life and Death of an American River.* New York: Crown Publishers, 1994.

———, ed. *The Sierra Club Desert Reader: A Literary Companion.* San Francisco: Sierra Club Books, 1995.

Medawar, P. B., and J. S. Medawar. *Aristotle to Zoos: A Philosophical Dictionary of Biology.* Cambridge: Harvard University Press, 1983.

Morris, Desmond. *The Mammals.* London: Hodder and Stoughton, 1965.

Nabhan, Gary Paul, ed. *Counting Sheep: Twenty Ways of Seeing Desert Bighorn.* Tucson: University of Arizona Press, 1994.

O'Flaherty, Wendy, ed. *Hindu Myths.* Harmondsworth: Penguin, 1975.

Phillips, John A. "Rhythms of a Desert Lizard." *Natural History,* October 1995.

Platonov, Andrei. *The Fierce and Beautiful World.* Translated by Joseph Barnes. New York: Dutton, 1971.

Prejevalsky, Nikolai. *From Kulja, Across the Tian Shan to Lob-Nor.* London: Sampson Low, Marston, Searle & Rivington, 1879.

Quammen, David. *The Song of the Dodo: Island Biogeography in an Age of Extinctions.* New York: Scribner, 1996.

Robin, P. Ansell. *Animal Lore in English Literature.* London: John Murray, 1932.

Rossabi, Morris. "All the Khan's Horses." *Natural History,* October 1994.

Rowland, Beryl. *Animals with Human Faces: A Guide to Animal Symbolism.* Knoxville: University of Tennessee Press, 1973.

Sax, Boria. *The Parliament of Animals: Anecdotes and Legends from Books of Natural History, 1775–1900.* New York: Pace University Press, 1992.

Sebeok, Thomas A., ed. *How Animals Communicate.* Bloomington: Indiana University Press, 1977.

Selous, Frederick Courtney. *African Nature Notes and Reminiscences.* London: Macmillan, 1908.

Seton, Ernest Thompson. *Wild Animals I Have Known.* New York: Charles Scribner's Sons, 1898.

Shenon, Sydney. "Battling over a National Symbol." *New York Times,* July 10, 1995.

Shepard, Paul. *The Others: How Animals Made Us Human.* Washington, D.C.: Island Press, 1996.

_____. *Thinking Animals.* New York: Viking, 1978.

Skutch, Alexander. *The Minds of Birds.* College Station: Texas A&M University Press, 1996.

Stanley, Alessandra. "Noble Steed Gallops Back from the Soviet Abyss." *New York Times,* November 11, 1995.

Steinbeck, John. *The Log from the Sea of Cortez.* New York: Viking, 1941.

Thomas, Elizabeth Marshall. *The Harmless People.* New York: Vintage, 1965.

Tuan, Yi-Fu. *Dominance and Affection: The Making of Pets.* New Haven: Yale University Press, 1984.

Tweit, Susan J. *The Great Southwest Nature Factbook.* Seattle: Alaska Northwest Books, 1992.

van Lawick-Goodall, Jane, and Hugo van Lawick. *Innocent Killers.* London: Collins, 1970.

Waddell, Helen. *Beasts and Fathers.* London: Constable, 1934.

Waldbauer, Gilbert. *Insects through the Seasons.* Cambridge: Harvard University Press, 1996.

Watson, Lyall. *Dark Nature: A Natural History of Evil.* New York: HarperCollins, 1996.

Weiner, Jonathan. *The Beak of the Finch.* New York: Alfred A. Knopf, 1994.

Werner, Floyd, and Carl Olson. *Insects of the Southwest.* Tucson: Fisher Books, 1994.

White, David Gordon. *Myths of the Dog-Man.* Chicago: University of Chicago Press, 1991.

White, T. H. *The Bestiary.* New York: G. P. Putnam's Sons, 1954.

Wilbur, Sanford R., and Jerome A. Jackson. *Vulture Biology and Management.* Berkeley: University of California Press, 1983.

Williams, Clayton. *Animal Tales of the West.* San Antonio: Naylor, 1974.

Wilson, Edward O. *The Insect Societies.* Cambridge: Harvard University Press, 1971.

Zeuner, Frederick E. *A History of Domesticated Animals.* New York: Harper & Row, 1963.

Ziolowski, Jan M. *Talking Animals: Medieval Latin Beast Poetry, 750–1150.* Philadelphia: University of Pennsylvania Press, 1984.

Index